The Executive Entrepreneur

5 Key Executive Coaching Shifts That Will Unleash Performance in Your Business Teams, Create Outstanding Leadership and Drive Innovation and Growth

by

Kevin Rennie

Amazon #1 Best Selling Book
in 7 Countries and 28 Categories

evolve Global Publishing
www.evolveglobalpublishing.com.au

Website: www.theexecutiveentrepreneur.com
Email: kevin.rennie@brightlingadvisory.com
Phone: 07770 700 743

Ordering Information: Quantity sales. Special discounts are available on multiple purchases by corporations, associations, and others.

For details, contact the "Special Sales Department" at the address above.

--1st edition, 2017
First Published 2017 for by Evolve Global Publishing
PO Box 327 Stanhope Gardens NSW 2768
info@evolveglobalpublishing.com
www.evolveglobalpublishing.com
Book Layout: © 2017 Evolve Global Publishing

www.evolveglobalpublishing.com.au

ISBN: (Paperback) 978-1-64007-044-8
ISBN: (Hardcover) 978-1-64007-045-5
ISBN-13: (Createspace) 978-1546323181
ISBN-10: (Createspace) 154632318X
ISBN: (Smashwords) 9781370999224
ASIN: (Amazon Kindle): B01N5GYBG1

This book is available on Barnes & Noble, Kobo, Apple iBooks (digital), Google Books (digital)

Table of Contents

Foreword

As the former Executive Vice President of Saatchi & Saatchi [One of the world's leading Advertising Agencies with over 6,000 employees in 71 different nations] I never recommend anyone or anything lightly.

That said, I have no hesitation in giving a hearty 'Thumbs Up' to Kevin Rennie's new book: The Executive Entrepreneur.

Why?

Because I have invested years of my life dealing with hundreds of 'Serial entrepreneurs' and billion dollars companies worldwide.

These days I am busy creating a 9-figure company with the aim of 'ending child hunger in the industrialized world' and again I find myself dealing with many executive entrepreneurs who want to make a difference in the world.

Years of real-world experience has taught me how to spot great strategy from downright garbage.

And so if you are serious about taking control of your career, your business and your life and seeing more genuine breakthroughs than you can possibly imagine, then simply implement what you discover as you read this book.

Stephen Clarke
CEO RTG Marketing Group
http://www.rtgmarketinggroup.com

Kevin Rennie

Acknowledgements

This work has been born out of more than twenty years of personal development and the successful delivery of a wide range of tough and challenging projects with great clients. The people involved in this journey are too numerous to mention, but they know who they are and they will recognize many of the experiences and stories in this book.

The actual process of crafting and writing this book and bringing it to the point where you can take advantage of the shifts outlined within it involved a closer peer set of very supportive individuals. I would like to thank in particular:

- Nancy Pile, my editor - for all her support and encouragement to get the book finished.

- Jason P. Jordan and all at Barnum Media - for their support in shaping this book and getting it out into the world, so you can read it.

- My wife, Sarah, and two amazing daughters, Charlotte and Isobel - for putting up with the times when I disappeared into the study to write and for their enthusiasm and support for what I do.

- Eric Fleming - for his work on unleashing teams, his encouragement in my work, and his support for this project.

- The many people who have commented on drafts and brought a whole new level of richness and clarity to the work. There are many here, notably Myles McLelland, Drew Lindon, Andrew Gray, Hazel Brodie, Bernice Barry, Mike Rumble, James Hart, Maarten Raaijmakers, and Kevin Freedman.

Kevin Rennie

Introduction

Is This Book For You?

No matter where you are now in your career, you are still capable of much more than you think. It is mainly a question of desire. Ask yourself, "Do I really want to achieve more than I currently am, and will doing so bring me happiness?" If the answer to these questions is yes and if you are willing to focus and act consistently to implement the insights herein, then this book is for you.

If you implement the insights in this book, even in part, then I guarantee that you will see results and build momentum to change your life for the better. I can make this guarantee because I have spent two decades working to help people design and deliver change, and I have made sure that the framework in this book is underpinned with rock-solid neuroscience, behavioral psychology, and powerful consulting frameworks. This is what the Executive Entrepreneur's journey is all about: applying practical tools and approaches to achieve more and to bring more into the world of what you want to create.

And you want to create and extend yourself, not because you necessarily lack anything, but because you want to be able to give and do more, both for yourself and your peers, but also for your family and loved ones. You are a person who wants to bring more joy, success, and prosperity into the world through your work.

That is not to say that your life is currently a bed of roses. Many people start off their journeys to being successful entrepreneurs because they are in some degree of discomfort or pain. That's OK.

It is important to recognize and use this discomfort to encourage yourself to take action.

Here are a few starting points for the Executive Entrepreneur's journey that you might recognize:

> *You work exceptionally hard in your business, putting in long hours and doing all the right things, but you know that you and your colleagues are capable of achieving more. You feel that you are not achieving your full potential and that your business is underperforming as a result. You are hungry for more success, but not quite sure how to get it.*

> *You manage a large portfolio of services, projects, and programs. You tackle complex challenges and deliver. And yet you feel that sometimes you don't get the recognition that your efforts deserve, and this causes you concern for your future career.*

> *You find that internal systems, corporate culture, or even sometimes your colleagues can create blocks and challenges that get in your way. You think, "It shouldn't be this hard to get things done. Why is the organization fighting me when we need to survive, we need to grow?"*

These are common starting points for many as they search for the keys to unlock performance and drive their businesses forward. The five shifts that I outline in this book lie within everyone's grasp, so don't worry if you are currently feeling frustrated or overwhelmed. The keys to gaining control and creating momentum are in your hands right now.

It also doesn't matter how senior you are. I work primarily with chief executives and other senior executives, and they are all grappling with one or more of the shifts we work through below. You may already have decades of experience under your belt, but unless you understand, practice, and live these fundamentals, you won't make the progress you deserve. Once you make these shifts, you'll be amazed at what you can achieve in a very short space of time. You will find that you can deliver results consistently that mark you and your organization out amongst the best in the world.

You will be well-placed to help lead your organization through the changes and transitions it needs to make in order to survive and grow in the increasingly fragmented global economy, an economy in which change and innovation are the only certainties businesses face.

By making these shifts, you will take control of your priorities and exercise choice over the projects that you work on and how you spend your time. And because you are deciding positively about your future, you will feel much more engaged and focused on making change happen. This will create the passion and drive that will enable you to lead change and growth successfully. You will be saying, "I'm ready for this. It's my time now."

You'll also find that the Executive Entrepreneur shifts apply to many other aspects of your life too. As you learn how to achieve more at work, you will also be able to apply some of the same tools and techniques to achieving more in other aspects of your life. You'll be able to generate the income you deserve, build an even more joyous home life, and enjoy great times with friends and families.

So read on. It's going to be great fun, and I'm already enjoying working with you.

Why I Wrote This Book

My great joy in life is helping other people succeed and being a part of that journey. I've been lucky enough to help improve the education of millions of young people. I have helped leaders tackle some of the most challenging national and global transformation programs being delivered right now. And I have the privilege of working directly with ambitious and talented leaders to help them achieve their dreams. Each one of these leaders has added insight and depth to my own perspective, and it is for them and for you that I have written this book. My passion is in helping you and others like you achieve your goals, and my firm belief is that with the right support, of which this book is only a part, you will get there. So dream big, have faith, and read on.

I am also writing this book because I am frustrated that so much of the leadership development training and literature out there is misguided and mediocre. You are ambitious, hungry, and keen to deliver. You've probably read many management books and watched many of the videos and webinars available on the Internet. And you will have worked out that there are a lot of people making false promises. The world is on fire with digital media, and so much different information is available to you. It can be hard to sort the wheat from the chaff. My aim is to help you cut through that by sharing my practical and first-hand experience of what works in simple, straightforward steps that anyone can follow.

My third motivation was to share some of my journey and the insights I have gathered (and continue to gather) along the way. I have had to make a number of career shifts as the economy and the world has changed, and I have learned a lot in doing so. I moved from the safe haven of being a highflying civil servant in the British government into the commercial world.

I worked in a number of the big consultancies, including KPMG, Capgemini, and PA Consulting at partner level, before setting up on my own. That experience gave me a huge amount of insight, resource, know-how and tool sets to draw on. And I had the privilege of working with hundreds of high-caliber executives on three separate continents, helping them fast-track their careers and transform the performances of their teams and organizations. All that work is really what enabled me to discover and crystallize the shifts that I present in this book.

I have found that while there may be specific knowledge that is relevant to your particular business, it's not the key to the successful Executive Entrepreneur's performance. In the data-driven information age we now live in, it is not knowledge that defines and marks the successful Executive Entrepreneur, but rather their mindset, skillset, and peer set that define their success, and these are developed and shaped in the fire of experience. I wanted to share some of my experiences and the experiences of those I have worked with and studied, with a view to helping you along your journey.

How to Use This Book

The Executive Entrepreneur framework set out in this book is simple, instantly understandable, and available to all. Your challenge lies in applying it. All the knowledge in the world is useless unless it is acted on. And so you need to act. Applied well, the exercises in this book will help you reach a significantly higher level of performance. You'll be able to keep raising your performance bar, day after day, week after week, and year after year for as long as you want to keep growing and keep giving to the world. After all, better never ends!

This book has been designed using what I call a "spiral curriculum," in which I aim to give you the topline picture quickly and then deepen your understanding of the principles as we go through.

The book is also designed to be used alongside your own journaling and the Executive Entrepreneur workbook, which you can download at www.theexecutiveentrepreneur.com/workbook. It is short enough to be read quickly in one sitting, but the real benefit will come when you use it as a framework and a guide in your daily practice.

I have included a series of Executive Entrepreneur challenges to help you deepen your understanding of the principles outlined in this book and to apply them in a very real and practical way to the challenges you face at work. It is not necessary to apply yourself to all of the given challenges to get value from this book. (I realize that there are quite a few of them!) However, you will face a wide variety of challenges, so my aim in writing this book is to ensure that you have a toolkit to help you think through and tackle them. How many of these exercises you choose to try out and put into practice straightaway is up to you.

My hope is that you engage with at least half of them within the next month or so, as you work through how to take your journey as an Executive Entrepreneur to the next level.

If you want to go farther on this journey, you may also want to think about joining one of my executive coaching groups. Here you will meet like-minded individuals and have a chance to share and work through challenges together. Again you can find out more about these at www.theexecutiveentrepreneur.com. The Executive Entrepreneur framework set out in this book is simple, instantly understandable, and available to all.

Your challenge lies in applying it. All the knowledge in the world is useless unless it is acted on. And so you need to act. Applied well, the exercises in this book will help you reach a significantly higher level of performance. You'll be able to keep raising your performance bar, day after day, week after week, and year after year for as long as you want to keep growing and keep giving to the world. After all, better never ends!

If you want to go farther on this journey, you may also want to think about joining one of my executive coaching groups. Here you will meet like-minded individuals and have a chance to share and work through challenges together. Again you can find out more about these at *www. theexecutiveentrepreneur.com.*

Take Your Journey Farther!

Download your FREE workbook, join one of my coaching groups, meet like minded individuals, and work through challenges together!

Find out more at:
www.theexecutiveentrepreneur.com

Chapter 1 - The Executive Entrepreneur's Framework

You are an amazing human being. You've done amazing things, but you have so much more to do and achieve. If you are reading this book, then I know you want more: you want to break through to even higher levels of performance, and you want to be able to achieve more of your full potential and to share that with others.

But you may not yet understand that there are two routes people take towards achieving this higher level of performance: the traditional, corporate development route, which is littered with failures and burnouts, and the Executive Entrepreneur's route, which, if you apply faithfully, will always work. Let me explain this seemingly outrageous claim.

Both routes start out with the same basic truth: that you are capable of way more than you think and way more than you have already achieved. Your current performance is defined simply by your current performance. No matter how great you are, that is your current level. But your potential performance is much greater, no matter whether you believe it or not. As Henry Ford pointed out, "Whether you think you can or whether you think you can't - you're right". Again, no matter how great you are now, your potential performance is much greater.

Case Study: Gina Bradbury

Late one recent summer, with very little fanfare, the University and Colleges Admissions Service (UCAS) opened its online doors to every 14 to 19 year old learner in England and Wales. Better known for its application service for university entrants, UCAS had decided it could better serve all learners by covering all learning opportunities open to young people, including non-university options, like colleges, apprenticeships, and work-based learning.

The organization had already scanned for opportunities and established a foothold in this new market, reaching about twenty percent of sixteen year olds in the country, and the chief executive, Mary Curnock Cook, knew that her team had the potential to transform services for young people in terms of how they think about and access a wider range of educational opportunities.

She invited me in to work closely with the head of the new service, Gina Bradbury, to focus their strategy and help them take action to make it a national success. Together we had scanned the market, assessed the business options, and focused the business strategy on growth by enabling wider and easier access to the service. We acted by revamping the technology and loading details on every relevant course in the country. Additionally, we engaged a fantastic range of stakeholders to make the service rich and exciting. In short, we created a new powerhouse of growth and transformation, sharpening the organization's focus on how to better serve a wider range of customers. And we had taken all the necessary action within six months of getting board approval to proceed.

Those six months of focused action were a fantastic experience. The organization rallied around the cause of enabling young people to make better choices, which was Gina's burning platform for change. We transformed the service options for 14 to 19 year olds from a rough coal into a sparkling jewel.

We transformed a service covering only parts of the country to one that is now available nationally, to every young person no matter his or her postcode. A service that had offered restricted learner accounts was now universally available. A service that had been viewed as a sideshow was now leading the way within the organization for customer-focused change.

What a shift! Gina is now one of the leaders of digital-age services in the UK, and, I would argue, globally. She helped drive her organization farther and faster as they gathered momentum and found more ways to better serve their customers.

Looking back, remarkable though this transformation was, there was no chance involved. We worked systematically and strategically through all the key challenges that Gina and her team faced to achieve multiple breakthroughs and shifts in performance through design and hard work. We used the framework in this book to create the insights and drive that enabled Gina to create momentum, transform delivery, and mark herself out for leading wider change within the organization.

You can do the same.

The Traditional Route to Boosting Performance

Assuming that your organization is ambitious and that your personal motivation and values are aligned in some way with that, it is likely that your company will offer you some form of support and opportunity to grow. If not, then you need to read Chapter Two at least twice - but let's stay focused here and look at the traditional way that organizations develop their people and how individuals carve out their careers in that context.

ONE - The first thing that typically happens is that they load you up. They give you a bunch of jobs and tasks that are intended to help you stretch and grow. The organization says, "Hey, here's a new opportunity. I want you to take it on." And because you are ambitious, the temptation is to say, "Sure, that's great! Thanks so much for the opportunity.

I'm the right person for the job, and I'll show you just how much we can achieve!" And you'll say that even if they don't always take other tasks and roles away from you to create the space you need to deliver or even when they do not give the resources you need to succeed. You say yes because you are ambitious, you want to make a difference, and you want to prove yourself.

You've heard the commonly used phrase: "If you want a job done, give it to a busy person," and there is truth in that. But it's also the first warning signal that you're in the traditional frame of personal and organizational development, which we know is littered with burned-out individuals, failed projects, and insolvent or struggling businesses.

TWO - The second thing that happens in the traditional model, if you are lucky, is that a leader will recognize some of this and decide, "Fine. We'll give you some skills training." And you think, "Great.

At least I'll have some opportunity to develop my skills as I go. And that should help me succeed." But don't be too hasty here.

What also commonly happens is that the training is delivered in a training room somewhere, or via an online course or at some institution, and you get some value from it, but it's not followed up effectively. It is often academic, generic, and one step removed from the reality of your organization: the trainer has designed large chunks of it to be rolled out "off the shelf," and you may struggle to find the full relevance or application to what you're doing. It's not always that bad, but there is a pattern of offering training courses that don't really meet your needs and don't create lasting change in your ability to deliver.

THREE - The third thing that happens is that the organization fails to give you adequate coaching and mentoring. This means that you are not able to grow rapidly into your new challenges, and you are not able to learn effectively from other people's experiences, successes, and failures. Even where organizations do offer you a coach or mentor, that person is likely to come from inside the organization because it helps to keep costs down. And while there are some great in-house mentors and coaches (and you should look for sponsorship from them), you may find yourself holding back somewhat in fear that other people around are judging you. Internal mentoring can lead to a mentee thinking, "I can't be totally open and transparent about this because I can't learn and fail in such a public way."

We will come back to establishing great coaching and mentoring in the fourth chapter. For now, I just want to flag that it is common for organizations to chuck resources down this route without fully understanding what is needed and how to get the most out of the invaluable resource of coaching or mentoring.

This is the traditional route to boosting performance, and it can be summarized in the following diagram.

Diagram 1: The traditional route to performance improvement

Accepting new opportunities to grow and stretch your performance is key to growth and achieving greater things. But if you are working within this traditional model of performance improvement, the support mechanisms put around you actually serve to constrain and hinder your achieving your full potential, rather than enhancing it.

There are only twenty-four hours in a day, and if you're being loaded up and working harder and harder to deliver on your increased portfolio, that generally leads in one direction: frustration, disillusionment, and ultimately burnout.

How many executives or aspiring executives do you know in this place? Even those who think they are in control and managing their work and stress levels effectively get caught by this, with increasing amounts of low-level illnesses, unexplained headaches, or even seizures and heart attacks.

We are the first generation that will not live as long as our parents' generation - and it is not just because of our diet. It is because of our lifestyles, the pressures of work, and how we respond to those.

If the traditional route to performance improvement is not the way to sustained, high-impact performance, economic growth, and prosperity, then things have to change. You have to move to a better and more sustainable framework for getting things done. Whether or not your organization is beginning to make these shifts, you have to take control of the situation yourself. And you can, whether it is within your company or beyond.

If you are part of the leadership team within your organization, your adopting the Executive Entrepreneur framework and the five shifts that are embedded within it has the power to transform your organization. Depending on the maturity of your organization, many of these elements may already be implicitly or explicitly embedded within its culture, values, and performance management framework. But, as with all fundamentals, it pays dividends to revisit and ensure your mastery of them. Take time to work through the framework within this book and also question whether and how your company can improve on its current ways of working and culture by taking the elements of this framework and incorporating them within your organization.

And regardless of your position within your company, you can apply this framework to improve your own performance. Many of you may be reading this book and thinking it's time to move companies. You know that most people move jobs several times in their careers now, whether through enforced redundancies or choice. That is the nature of the economic world we operate in now, and it is a good thing. It enables the new to replace the old, the fresh thinking to replace the worn-out, and the drive for growth and regeneration to continue.

But you don't have to leave your job for this growth and regeneration to take place. Because the truth is that you are in control. You decide your future.

You decide how you operate in each and every situation, and while the stresses and strains of your current situation may have crowded out this truth, it remains true. So whatever your situation and however much stress you are under, let this book be your guide. It will help you find your own answers to where you can improve your performance and unlock your potential.

Just the simple fact that you are reading this book is an indication that you are on the path. You are hungry for growth. You are keen to explore other people's ideas and insights, and incorporate them into your own. So keep reading and remember to apply the knowledge and exercises in this book. In this way you will be able to take control, regardless of your situation and no matter how strong or weak your current performance.

The Executive Entrepreneur Framework

Great entrepreneurial performance is all about growth and making a significant contribution to the organization. It can take hard work, but if you work in the right way with the right tools, support, and advice, you will be able to make significant contributions time and time again. I know because I've experienced it myself, and I've consistently helped others make similar progress. It's an exciting, challenging, and rewarding journey.

Part One

The journey always begins with three simple words: Scan, Focus, and Act. And we apply these to three areas of our performance: our mindset, our skillset, and our peer set. Applied faithfully, correctly, and consistently, greatness becomes possible. For greatness is already within us: we just have to find the keys to release it. And this framework provides those keys. Here it is in diagram form.

Diagram 2: The Executive Entrepreneur's Framework

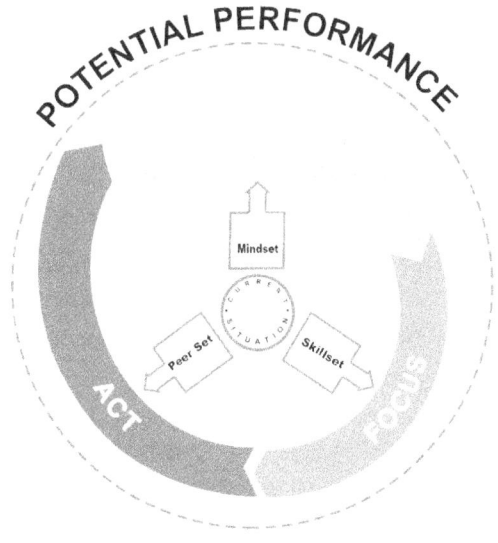

The truly exciting thing about this approach to developing yourself is that your potential for growth really holds no bounds, other than the limits you place on yourself.

This simple framework also encapsulates the core essence of any truly successful change process. Any other approach to change fits within this model, often in part and seldom in full. It is incredibly powerful once you get to grips with it. I've used it successfully with individuals, executive teams, and global networks. Through its application, we have enabled teams to make six months of progress in two days. And crucially, I have applied it to my own business and coaching of clients as we work together to achieve our goals. It is elegant, simple, and it works.

Scan, focus, and act is a journey: one that we all recognize and take every day in many, many different ways. When we encounter a challenging situation at work, we scan for what is going on: what led to this challenge, what factors we know, what we don't, and what situations we have experienced in the past that we can draw on. Sometimes we scan less than we should, and sometimes our brains do so subliminally as we react in the moment. But scan we do.

Then, immediately after the scanning, we narrow down our options and evaluate the correct course of action. Again, we may do this quickly or slowly, depending on the complexity of the situation, our experience, and the pressure we are under. But again, focus we must if we are to do anything coherent.

And with that focus, we then step into action. Without action, nothing happens. Nothing changes. Even deciding to do nothing is an action. Action is a necessity. And the clarity and focus we bring to our actions depends on the quality of the preceding steps in which we scanned and focused.

The framework is simple and has the benefit of being universally applicable: we scan, we focus, and we act. Doing so deliberately gives us choice and control over our actions.

So for now, focus on raising your awareness of this process in the decisions you face at work and how you decide to act. Just raising your awareness and considering whether you have fully understood the situation (scanned correctly) or whether you have focused down clearly enough on the correct course of action can help.

Part Two

The second part of the framework addresses the three areas of content: our mindset, our skillset, and our peer set. We'll explore each of these areas carefully in Chapters Two to Four, but to start, let's have a quick look at how the whole model fits together.

Case Study: Richard Branson

Richard Branson is a big source of inspiration to so many people. He's created an amazingly strong brand within his own lifetime and achieved so many things with that. But I want to go right back to the beginning. In the 1960s, Branson wasn't into records as a business. He started by publishing Student, a magazine run by and for students. I'm going to show how he used the Scan-Focus-Act model to move from there into what he is now doing.

When publishing Student, Branson was having fun and doing really great work. He was interviewing people, like Mick Jagger and R.D. Laing, putting together great stories, and making sure that the magazine sold well and that ads were in it as well. He likely knew that it wasn't what he was going to do forever, so all the while, he was scanning, looking for other promising possibilities.

When he saw a niche in the market for mail-order records, he focused and acted swiftly using many aspects of the Executive Entrepreneur's mindset that I outline in Chapter Two. For example, he moved out of his comfort zone of running Student into the more unknown territory of the music business.

He reduced the risk by testing the market first, including ads for mail-order music in his own magazine and in this way managed to start a different business underneath which he flipped straight into Virgin Records. He learned new skills, like how to open shops without having to pay rent for three months, and within a couple of years, he'd gone from publishing Student to running a recording studio that had acquired some massive names too - Mike Oldfield for one. He had a significantly different peer set around him from the start of his venture, and from there, it grew.

Branson was scanning - looking at the environment. When he saw the big opportunity, he focused in on it, and crucially, he took action. And not only did he take action, but he did so with increasing velocity. He was able to make decisions fast and then acted swiftly, accelerating right through whatever fear and doubt he may have been experiencing. He constantly checked to make sure he had things going for him and made adjustments where he needed to. He was always very conscious about cash flow and savvy about how he positioned the new Virgin front stores, making sure that he got cheap leases for the first period of landing the space - sometimes even saying, "Give us a space for free, and we'll pay you when we've made a profit." He was very careful to make sure that his business remained successful. He was transformative. It was one of the most exciting years in British music, and Branson rode that crest, signing the labels, creating the record label, and from there, moving on.

Again, if you look at the recent cycle he's been through - once he consolidated his position around Virgin Atlantic, he then exploded onto the scene with multiple brands. He now owns over 200 companies worldwide, and he's doing amazing things, forming alliances with new people to spin out numerous new businesses - another major Scan-Focus-Act cycle.

Unpacking the Executive Entrepreneur Framework

Let's turn now to look at each step in the Scan-Focus-Act framework, understand it in more detail, and look at how it can be applied practically to you and your situation.

Scan

When making decisions, it is common to use instinct or intuition and drive straight to focusing on the decision. What people are really doing is using their experiences and their subconscious minds to undertake a very rapid scanning phase that enables them to focus quickly and move forwards. But a conscious and deliberate scanning phase can often help you make better decisions, for a number of reasons.

First, when making decisions, most people decide on a polarized basis: yes or no? Option A or B? This is black-and-white decision-making, but we know that the world has more than fifty shades of gray - which is why we polarize. We don't like so many choices, and our brains get addled when given too much. The subconscious mind also likes these kinds of two-option decisions because it has lots of experience to draw on and is able to say "Course A because . . ."

However, it often helps to slow your decision-making a bit. Look around, take your time, and make sure you have a decent range of options to choose from. If you are choosing between two courses of action, then you are not really choosing. It's only when three or more options are on the table that you begin weighing things more carefully and exercising your judgment about what is best. This is all about scanning. I use the following acronym to guide me:

S – Search

Look for opportunities to improve. Read. Ask your customers, staff, and board members about what needs to happen next.

Look outside your organization at what is happening elsewhere. Be expansive and open to things you have not thought about before.

C – Collate

Gather together the key information and sift it into a format that works best for you. There are many tools, including mind maps, spreadsheets, presentations, vision boards, or your personal journal, to name just a few. Just pick the one that works best for you and start collating your thoughts in one place.

A – Assess

Set aside time to think. What have you learned so far? What is it telling you?

N – New

What's new here? What's missing? What more do you need to think about?

Success Tips for Scanning

To help you apply the Scan phase in your own life and work:

- **Use scanning as the first step in goal setting.** While we dig into this more deeply in Shift 1, a top tip for now is to let your mind and ambition roam widely. Look at all aspects of your life and career as you think about what goals you want to set for yourself. Decisions for focusing and acting come next. For now enjoy yourself: think broadly and be ambitious. If you don't start off open to what might be, how can you expect to be able to focus and act towards achieving great things?

- **Be methodical but not labored.** Work through the scan phase quickly but thoroughly to make sure you have a full picture of the opportunities for change. For example, in meetings don't be too quick to jump to solutions. Spend some time understanding the problem and looking at whether you have all the information you need before moving on to finding a fix for the problem. This need not be arduous, but it is an important step in making sure you have genuine choices to focus on. Even where there is pressure within your organization to move fast, don't skip the scan phase of your work. Remember that a choice is not really a choice unless you have at least three options to choose from, and be sure to engage your seniors in this stage of the work so that they are sighted and not subjected to the "grand reveal" when you come to present your findings.

Focus

For Focus, I like the total quality management acronym, which has stood the test of time. I have extended it to make it to cover a wider set of reminders about what to address during this phase.

F – Find an Opportunity to Improve

From your work in the Scan phase, what are the most promising opportunities to make improvements?

O – Organize an Effective Team

Who else might you discuss this with? Who can help you achieve your objectives? Think both inside and outside your team, and also inside and outside your organization. Do you need a coach or consultant to bring a fresh perspective or facilitate faster progress?

C – Clarify

What are the main options for moving forwards? Narrow these down to a manageable number and, crucially, clarify them. What is involved in making the shift? What are the costs and benefits?

U – Understand

Understand what might go wrong. What can you do to minimize these risks? Understand what the upside is and how you can maximize that.

S – Select

Select the best option based on the information available. Plan and thoroughly think through what needs to be done so that when you act, you do so with ruthless effectiveness.

Success Tips to Focus

To focus effectively in your own life and work:

- **Recognize where deeper thinking is required.** Some changes will be obvious, and you can quickly focus, but others require further work, a deeper dive, in order to get clarity. This requires patience and application. As the Nobel Prize winner Daniel Kahneman noted in his influential book Thinking, Fast and Slow, it is only where we have deep knowledge and understanding of a situation that we can be more certain that our intuition is solid. More often than not, we need to slow down and take a more careful look at the situation. We must recognize that we are in a cognitive minefield and ask for reinforcement by engaging consciously and weighing up the situation carefully. As the widely used prayer reminds us:

  O God, give us the serenity to accept what cannot be changed, The courage to change what can be changed, And the wisdom to know the one from the other.

- **Ask other people for their perspectives.** Particularly, ask your customers as well as your colleagues. Many businesses struggle to engage their customers in product and service development, and fail to gather the insights that listening to them can yield.

Try, as much as possible, to get your customers to be open and honest about what they think, and share these findings with your colleagues. Explore carefully what is going on and think about the challenges that your customer feedback suggests you must tackle. There is an old saying, "Before you judge a person, you must walk a mile in their shoes." This applies as much to business as it does to relationships.

- ***Don't accept conventional wisdom.*** Think different. Dr. Edward de Bono's "Six Thinking Hats" exercise can be great for this - where you either imagine or even wear hats of different colors that symbolize and prompt different ways to think about and respond to a certain situation or problem.

- ***Ask whether you are focusing on the right thing.*** Often, I have found when working with clients that the initial problem is not the real one - it is just the first barrier that they perceive. Often it is something else behind this that is the real need for change. For example, an executive I was working with was concerned that his line manager was overly controlling on minor decisions, such as signing off on small business development expenses. The root of the problem, it turned out, was much more fundamental: the line manager was using these details to divert focus from the rather more serious challenge of bringing in sufficient sales to close the year on budget. Once this was recognized, the executive I was working with was easily able to take appropriate action to tackle the real issue.

Act

Action is really where your work starts to become tangible. What you've been doing up to this point is prologue. You now need to act and act fast. Don't wait for tomorrow. Start today, even with a small, simple step.

A – Accelerate

It's all about momentum: what can you do right now? Don't worry about taking huge steps. If you can, that's fantastic, but momentum is all about getting started. Don't take too long in the Scan or Focus phase; you can do both very quickly, within a week or two, even faster if you need to.

C – Commit, Check, and Change

Act with conviction. Make sure you're moving in the right direction. Make adjustments if necessary.

T – Transform

Be the best version of you: breakthrough that performance barrier and push hard for the results you need most.

Remember, and this is worth repeating: it's all about focus and momentum. You've probably already been taking action, but the key is to take action in a focused, coherent way. This builds momentum. Without focus, you won't hit your target.

Success Tips for Action

To help you act effectively in your own life and work:

- ***Take small and immediate actions.*** Small actions lead to bigger ones. So think about doing things as simple as the following:

    - Put on your running shoes and start now with a walk or jog around the block.

    - Write an email to reach out to your business partner with a new idea for action.

○ Book that restaurant for dinner with your partner, and, if necessary, organize the babysitter so that you have couple time and the chance to connect and share your ambitions for the next period of your life.

Small commitments such as these can make a big difference in the quality of your life and work. Your internal dialogue alone is not going to be enough; you need to keep building momentum. You have to act. You don't even need to have full clarity at this stage because you're going to be able to check and re-balance to make sure you're moving in the right direction. But you must decide to act. And when you do act, you must act with conviction. Have no doubt that you are moving forwards towards the outcomes that you so badly want.

- **Make public commitments.** Find ways to commit to what you're doing in some way that holds you to account with other people because a public commitment is harder for you to wriggle out of. It's harder to say to others, "I tried, but it didn't work out," particularly if you put some personal pride at stake. Why not commit in public to your coach, teammates, spouse, or friends? This will force you to focus on success and motivate you to avoid the embarrassment and difficulty you would face from failing to follow through.

- **Use the two-minute rule.** One way of getting committed is to use the two-minute rule: do something quick that takes no more than two minutes and which commits and moves you towards your goal. For any bigger task there is a small and simple first step that creates momentum. It could be as simple as writing the first line of a document or creating the outline; it could be picking up the phone to call a colleague or arranging that date-night with your spouse that you've been meaning to get to. Small, simple tasks create momentum. Here are two that relate to the ideas in this book:

○ Download the workbook that goes with this book; and before you finish reading this book, go out and buy yourself a new, clean journal so that you can start the process of daily journaling. Downloading the workbook will take seconds, and buying the journal will take less than two minutes if you stop in at your local stationary store on the way back from work, or just buy it on online.

○ Once you have read this book and gathered your thoughts, you might arrange a review meeting with key people in your peer set to discuss the ideas you have to take your business forwards. Arranging that review meeting will take no more than two minutes.

Applying the Framework

The key to unlocking the power of this framework is to apply it repeatedly, keeping sight of the objective and using the approach it outlines in a flexible and creative way to make sure that the changes you want to make really do happen. Think of it like a magnifying glass used to kindle fire to a piece of paper. The sunlight can't burn paper the paper without the magnifying glass, but you need to move it in and out, to find the point of focus, before the paper ignites. This framework is the magnifying glass, but you need to apply it to the opportunities you have to make a difference. Applied intelligently, you will ignite your performance.

You can also apply the framework to all walks of life. While I have focused this book on the Executive Entrepreneur's challenges in the work place, the neuroscience underpinning it is sound and will work in any other aspect of your life. In particular, pay close attention to the Focus stage. By focusing, we harness our subconscious to carry on scanning. We program something in the brain called the reticular activating system when we clarify and focus on a goal. By creating a clear focus that we can retain and recall in the conscious mind, we transfer that focus also to the subconscious mind which filters billions of bits of data each day and only renders up to the conscious mind those bits that we will find useful.

Because we have told the subconscious mind what to look for, in creating our focus, it renders up information and opportunities that will help us achieve the goal on which we focus. This is the reticular activating system at work. Some of the "New Age" self-help literature talks about this as the "law of attraction," but in my view this "law" is founded in the physical world and arises because we have allowed ourselves to become sufficiently focused on the specific goals that we desire.

It is also interesting to note that any consulting or business model can fit into this framework, either in part or in full. Some models expand more on the Scan stage, some on the Focus stage, and some of the Act stage. Few are well balanced across each stage of the Scan-Focus-Act model. So being aware of the overarching Scan-Focus-Act framework helps us take a balanced and clear view of the tools we are using to understand the opportunities at hand.

This fundamental process sits at the core of any human behavior, any decision, any change. That's why I want you to get very familiar with it and use it alongside the other tools that you are already familiar with. It brings clarity and momentum to any challenge because it is so simple and powerful and crucially, because it drives action rather than talk.

Executive Entrepreneur Challenge 1: Apply Scan-Focus-Act

In this first Executive Entrepreneur challenge I want you to relax and let go for a while. Trust the process and allow yourself to work through your challenges using the following two-step process that gets you straight into using the Executive Entrepreneur framework.

Step 1: De-clutter your mind.

Start with a "pre-scanning" stage. De-clutter your mind by writing down a long list of things that are annoying you, blocking you, or slowing you down at work. Now rest your mind on a specific challenge by sifting that long list into different categories and selecting one specific challenge to work with in this exercise. Pick something that is important to you on this day or week. Make it real. There will be a ton of other stuff that you could focus on, but I want you to pick one challenge that we can work on together and make progress on right now. For example, when my clients first do this exercise, they often focus on top line challenges such as identifying their top five goals for the year or clarifying the core element of their business plan for the year.

Once they are familiar with the framework, they apply it to other aspects of their work as a problem-solving tool. Remember that you can come back and repeat this exercise as many times as you want, so don't worry too much about picking the most important. Just pick one that is relevant and on which you feel you can make progress.

Step 2: Apply the model.

Begin this part of the challenge with three blank sheets of paper (or use those in the workbook provided for this exercise). Write at the top of each piece of paper what the challenge is. Describe it in a few words or a sentence or two, something that makes clear to you and anyone reading the page what you are working on. Our aim in working through this exercise will be to create some specific and focused actions that will help you move towards sorting the challenge out and help you begin to get used to the process of applying the Scan-Focus-Act framework.

Underneath the description, write SCAN on the first page, FOCUS on the second page, and ACT on the third. These three pages now form the framework for capturing your thoughts.

Now I simply want you to work through the model outlined above:

- **Scan:** Search your mind for what is going on. Brainstorm this for five minutes, and then take a step back from this picture to assess what you are discovering. Ask yourself if there are any new or different perspectives that you can bring to the situation: what would your colleagues say? What would a board member say? Using the elements of the tried and trusted PESTEL framework (political, environmental, social, technological, economic, legal) as prompts may also shed new light. You can also often find different perspectives even within your mind's own internal dialogue.

- *Focus:* Once you are happy that you have a broad perspective from the scanning stage, move on to the questions set out in the Focus stage of the framework. Who else around you can you draw on to help you understand that or move it forwards? Clarify what is going on. Write down all the different causes and effects in the situation. And finally, select one or more things that you can do to tackle the challenge. These might be short-, medium-, or long-term actions. We'll generate real-time action in the next stage - what I want you to do in this part of the exercise is just get clear on what actions you will take over a period of time to tackle the challenge.

- *Act:* Now you are ready to decide what are you going to do. From this analysis, select one or two key actions that will move you forwards. Commit to them, and imagine what the future will be like once these are achieved. To create momentum towards achieving them, find one or more smaller actions that you can take today to move you forward. And crucially, take one immediate action now. Go on... Stop thinking and start doing! That's it. Stop thinking now, put this book down, and go do it. Just do it!

Take Your Journey Farther!

Download your FREE workbook, join one of my coaching groups, meet like minded individuals, and work through challenges together!

Find out more at:
www.theexecutiveentrepreneur.com

Chapter 2 - Mindset

Your mindset is absolutely critical to achieving your goals. As with any program, to accomplish breakthrough results you can have the skills and the team around you, but if you have the wrong mindset, you're going nowhere. So that's where we start.

The following sections in this chapter distill for you the most important aspects of achieving that Executive Entrepreneur's mindset and show you how to apply them in practice to attain outstanding results at work. Work through this chapter carefully. Take time to apply the exercises and reflect. If you don't have one already, please buy a journal this week (see below) and use it to record your reflections and progress.

You can apply the same tools and techniques to your family life, your spiritual life, your financial wellbeing, or any other area of your life that you want to work on. However, because this book is about helping the Executive Entrepreneur achieve outstanding business performance, we are going to focus on how to install the Executive Entrepreneur's mindset in your work. This is the first shift you must make, and we explore it further below.

Shift 1: Adopt an Executive Entrepreneur's Mindset

This first shift, of adopting the right mindset is, without question, the most important shift that you must make if you are going to achieve beyond your current performance. You can do anything, but not everything. You are going to have to choose what to put your mind to. But know this one thing: you are powerful. You are capable beyond even your own dreams. It really is down to you, and fundamentally it is down to how you manage your mindset.

The most powerful mindset we can adopt is one in which we see things already done. We know the outcome that we want to achieve, we have pictured it in great detail, we have envisioned it, and we have seen it done. Looking back from this place of achievement, we can see the steps that we took along the way to make it so. That sounds a bit like Star Trek doesn't it? "Make it so, Number One!" Those words were not uttered idly. The Number One in question had made a suggestion and knew it could be done. All he needed was approval from his captain to make it so. And this was given.

So we reach the heart of the matter right at the outset. You are the master of your destiny. You are the captain of your soul. Everything that you do, everything that you think, everything that you say contributes to your destiny. So think, speak, and act carefully, from a mindset in which you see things done and you step out into the day with confidence.

Confidence may be overstating it a bit in terms of each and every day: we all have our moments of self-doubt. We must embrace these moments, recognize them as our friends, and move through them. Let's look at this in more detail.

Embrace Being Uncomfortable

If you're not stretching yourself, if you're not pushing yourself - you're not growing. If you're not uncomfortable, that's a signal that you need to be thinking about things in a different way, that you've got to push yourself outside your comfort zone to start to stretch and challenge yourself.

This is a wake-up call for those of you who find your job mundane or boring, and are frustrated because you're being passed over. It's almost certainly a sign that you're not doing enough to challenge and stretch yourself in your current position. If you're going to be a successful Executive Entrepreneur, if you're going to get to the next level in your career and your life, then you've got to push yourself beyond your comfort zone into the space that stretches your current level of performance and into the rare air that the people above you are breathing. And to do that, you make the most of the opportunities that you have right now to extend yourself.

It's only by going beyond your current level of performance that you're going to be able to learn and demonstrate more of what you're capable of. If you do, and if you apply the other shifts in this book, then when you look back in a year's time, or even in three months' time, you'll think, "I have achieved so much. I have gone way beyond what I thought was possible." My coaching point here to you is - get uncomfortable, so you can harness the discomfort that you need to drive yourself to new levels of achievement.

What that really means is that you have to take on new challenges, you have to get onto the biggest problems that your company faces - and you're going to have to crack them. If you're not on those projects already, you're going to have to ask to get on them.

If you're worried about how much time that's going to take, you've got to think about how you structure your day, how you structure your workload, and find ways through that.

There are no excuses here. You're going to have to ask to get on the biggest problems that your company faces and work through them. I've always been amazed what happens when people simply ask for opportunities. People are looking for ways to get things done. If you're offering a way through that, saying, "I can help here," people will usually accept that offer. If you're worried about your workload, then think about this: there are plenty people beneath you in your team that want to get into your shoes, so give them some opportunity to take on problems and challenges that you're tackling and give them some of your workload.

Here's another way of thinking about things too. If you were to go off sick for a day or two, or even a week, which often happens to executives who push themselves too hard, what is the worst that would happen? The world would still turn, people would cope and it is unlikely anybody would die. Sure, they might start to fill the space that you leave, which you might feel nervous about, but is that so bad? Is it awful that you're enabling others to fulfill bigger roles than their job descriptions set down? I know that's a bit of a hard message to take, but I'm challenging you here. That's my job! You've got to find ways of giving away some of your workload, which feels so precious and important to you, to other people. You've got to push down your tasks and activities so that you get to focus on what matters for your future, and other people get opportunities to grow and challenge themselves too. This is a virtuous spiral upwards, one which gives you the time and space to think and do things differently and enables you to unleash the full power of your team.

When things get tough - and they will get tough - you've got to find ways of looking at the challenges that you're facing as opportunities.

I know that is easy to say. I've worked with many executives who've been ready to resign and throw up their hands, lamenting, "This is just too much, I can't push this person or this team or this organization in the way that it needs to be pushed. It's fighting me too hard, and I can't take anymore."

That's a common fear or challenge that executives face. You've got to turn the fear and challenge around, and make it into something where you can say to the organization, "I'm going to show you how we can do things differently. I'm going to show how we can really bust through these things that are causing problems for us. I'm going to show us and everyone around us how we can get through it and take on those challenges."

There's a great saying, "Calm seas don't make good sailors." It's so true. If things are easy, if things are plain sailing, if the wind is behind you, the clients are rolling in, everything is great, and you're a hero - then that's fantastic. But when things get tough, you may not have built up the skills, the resilience, and the experience that enables you to find your way through the challenges. So if things are tough right now, then in one sense I'm asking you to celebrate that, to decide, "Okay, this is real tough, but I'm going to find the way through this. I'm going to find the way that is going to lift this organization to the next level and lift my performance to the next level."

Turn Negatives Into Positives

So many people are stuck in negative mindsets. They know exactly what they do not want but struggle to articulate clearly what they do want. And then they are surprised when they get exactly what they don't want. People stuck in this mindset find life frustrating. They know they want to be someplace else, but they can't quite bring that into reality.

One of the best ways to tackle this negative mindset is to turn your negative statements into positive ones. When you catch yourself about to say, "Don't do that," or words to that effect, try instead to find words to express what you do want. This is basic psychology, and it does work.

Let me illustrate with two examples. For those of you who have children or have seen parents struggle with certain aspects of the children's behavior think about this for a second. When you ask your children to stop arguing, you may often find that your request is either ignored or only adhered to for a very short space of time.

That is because you stated your request negatively - you asked them to stop doing something. Instead, you are much more likely to achieve a better outcome if you direct their attention to something more constructive. You might suggest that you play a game together, read a book with them, or do something more constructive than arguing. By stating what you want positively, you direct their attention to something constructive, so you are much more likely to get the outcome you want.

Similar dynamics play out in the workplace too. If you are unhappy at work, you can do one of two things. You can either focus on why you're unhappy and complain and moan about the situation, or you can choose to see the opportunity to make a positive decision to do something about it. Where you focus is where you choose to direct your energy; whatever you focus on, you are likely to get more of the same.

I'm not trying to suggest that one should paper over the cracks. If something is making you unhappy, you'd better understand why that is and do something about it: either change of circumstances or change your perspective. If you don't do one of these things, then you will be stuck in the same place, caught in a trap, doing the same thing over and over again but expecting different results.

Engage Your Heart

Life is too short for doing things that you don't really get passionate about. You've got to find the reason that you're showing up for work, and you've got to make sure that reason really is connected to your heart. If you can find that raison d'être, if you can find the passion in your work, then that is what is going to give you the edge that you need to stay on top of your game, to drive your business to new levels of success, and to really deliver an outstanding performance.

If your heart is not in it, you need to rethink. If you're not clear why you want to achieve higher levels of performance or if your reasons for doing so are not tapping into your heart's true desires, then I can't guarantee that you're going to achieve that success. If this is the case, you must either change your perspective so that your heart is in it, or try something else, something different. It's that simple.

Life is too short for drudgery, so don't be the richest person in the graveyard. Don't just do what you are used to. Push yourself, get engaged in things that you really feel passionate about, and engage your heart. That is what's going to give you the edge, that's what's going to enable you to embrace being uncomfortable and push yourself to the next level.

However, if you have thought deeply and clearly about your desires, if you know exactly why you're driving yourself to the next level, and if your motivation is in line with your deepest desires - then, with the right coaching and support, I can guarantee you will achieve the success you are seeking. It may take time, and it may come through in different ways to those you expected, but if you focus completely on succeeding on what matters to you most deeply, it will happen - provided you take consistent and appropriate action.

So how do you engage your heart fully in your quest for peak performance? Before I answer this question, I'd like to share another story that illustrates powerfully the importance of living a meaningful life.

If you haven't read it already, I thoroughly recommend Viktor Frankl's Man's Search for Meaning.

Case Study: Viktor Frankl

Frankl, a Jewish doctor, survived life in Auschwitz and other concentration camps by engaging his heart fully. He found rich meaning in the depths of the most traumatic and desperate situations that humans have ever managed to inflict on each other. His story is a lesson to us all.

He noticed, while in Auschwitz, that one of the key differences between those who lived and those who died was the individual's ability to be loving and kind and stand outside of his or her own desperate situation, at least for moments. Those who became self-absorbed, for example, in hoarding food or focusing on their own plights rather than helping and sympathizing with others, were the ones that struggled for meaning. And Victor found that those who struggled for meaning, sooner or later, faded away.

Victor proposes that this is because a life in which only you matter is not one of sufficient meaning to pull you through the toughest moments, moments where you need to dig to the deepest reserves that your soul can muster in order to survive, moments where you need the strength to endure what others might consider impossible to endure. Frankl gives some terribly graphic stories about how people would literally just give up, fade away, and die (though, of course, millions were also put to death who had not given up). One can only imagine how you or I might respond in similar circumstances.

Viktor was incredibly lucky too, with his position as a doctor and with the guards who helped him out. But he was also inspired and chose to interpret his situation differently and respond with strength and resolve. He engaged his heart. He found the ability to speak to others, inspiring and motivating them.

He shared or gave away his food, and promised himself that if he got through the horrors, he would do everything within his power to make sure that others would learn what he had learned so that the horrors would not be repeated. He found new meaning, and when the war eventually ended, he set up a new school of psychotherapy that is still influential to this day.

Viktor's story shows us that we can - and must - find meaning in our daily existence. We must set our sights on heights beyond our own material gain and success. We must strive for achievement beyond and outside our own self-gratification. If your ultimate goal, beyond becoming CEO or setting up your own business, is just to make a lot of money, is that really enough to sustain you through the sacrifices you will need to make? Is that enough to motivate you to maintain the single-minded focus that you will need to succeed?

The power of the human spirit when focused on the heart's true desires is literally unstoppable, as powerful as the sun, which feeds everything on this planet. Of course, there are bad things and bad people too, and we have to recognize and be realistic about that. But focus on what's right. Tap into that meaning, and within that, you will find your own personal power and the ability to achieve the highest levels of performance.

Executive Entrepreneur Challenge 2: Create Your Portrait of a Life Well-Lived

Let's forget your daily work for the moment and set aside ten minutes for this exercise. Are you ready? Good.

Now close your eyes and relax, and as you relax, look back from where you are today in your life, and give thanks for all the amazing things you've achieved so far. If bad stuff comes to mind, give thanks for it too: it has made you stronger and more capable. It formed this great person you now are. Give thanks for it and move on to the good stuff. Focus on the good, sensing it with your eyes, your ears, your skin, and your emotions, and give thanks.

Now from where you are today, wind forward time by thirty years or so, and imagine where you want to be. In your mind's eye, paint a portrait of a life well-lived and ask yourself these questions:

- What will you be doing?
- What have you achieved, and what are you most proud of?
- How did you spend your time?
- What will your family be like, and what will they be doing?
- What have you given to enable them to achieve their dreams?
- How do you feel?
- What friends will you have around you?
- Who will you be talking to?
- What will all these people think of you?
- What will they most admire about you?

Ask yourself other questions too - let your mind roam over the great things you have yet to achieve. I want you to create a really rich picture in your head of a life well-lived. Keep going for just a few more minutes and consider: what did you not do, as well as what did you do? It's very important to be very clear about what you didn't do because that is how you're going to create the space and time to achieve what you are aiming for. Ask yourself:

- What did you discard?
- What did you delegate?
- What did you drop?
- Who did you forgive?
- What did you not worry about?

And rather than finish on the negative, go back to the positive and recapture that. Focus on it to the exclusion of all else. Make it richer, bigger, brighter, louder. Turn up the volume on all those amazing things you have done. Really make it sing out to your heart - seeing it and feeling it.

Now capture this portrait in writing whilst it is fresh. Either write it down in your journal or speak it into the voice-recording app on your smart phone, recording all the things that you're grateful you did, achieved, saw, and felt. Connect with that "Portrait of a Life Well-Lived" and record it. If you've spoken it, then have your recording transcribed. Print out your portrait description and absorb it. Really tattoo that image on your brain and connect your heart and soul with it. Regularly revisit your written Portrait of a Life Well-Lived - even on a daily basis. Get familiar with that life that you are already creating.

Once you've done that, you need to connect what you are doing currently in your life to live your Portrait of a Life Well-Lived.

- How is your current work enabling you to achieve your life well-lived?

- Is it just providing you with money, or are there other things that your work gives you?

- Does it give you connection with other people, the chance to try new things and develop new skills, the opportunity to travel, the ability to lead and shape the future of your organization and how it serves its customers?

- What else does your work give you?

In this way, you should be able to see that your daily work is connecting you to the life you envision and are creating for yourself. You should be able to wake each morning looking forward to the day, thinking, "Fantastic - another opportunity to do even more to create the life I envision and am already living." And know that this is not some mental trick. This is reality.

If you can't connect your daily work in any way with the life you envision and are going to bring into reality, then you don't need me to tell you that you should take a good long look at what you are doing and consider your options for doing something different.

Act from Your Portrait of a Life Well-Lived

Once you've engaged your heart and articulated your Portrait of a Life Well-Lived, you need to cement it into your mindset. You need to live, act, and breathe as if it is already reality and you're just making it more real. That way, you can harness all the skills and energy you have within yourself to achieve it - both at conscious and subconscious levels.

When you make a decision, decide from the perspective of yourself in your Portrait of a Life Well-Lived. Get in touch with that version of yourself when you form relationships (or not) or decide to do something (or not). Be that ideal version of yourself in your present, in your now - this is the path to making the ideal a reality. Right now, through your mind, you can literally transform yourself. Make the effort; take the time to do it. Live through your ideal self.

If you have a very clear mental picture of what it is you want and you see it done, your subconscious mind will start to filter, to scan, looking for opportunities to bring it into reality. This might sound like a bit of New Age waffle, but it is based on neuroscience. Your subconscious brain is an incredibly powerful filtering machine, processing billions of bits of information each day and only serving up to your conscious brain the bits that matter.

You have to have that mental picture - and then write it down and connect with it on an emotional level.

- What are the things that you're going to feel as you are in this new place where this breakthrough performance is achieved?

- How are you going to be, how are you going to experience life at work, how will your colleagues perceive you?

See that place, be in that place, put yourself mentally in that place now. Get yourself into that state where you see it done.

A key aspect to forging the ideal self with your real self involves connecting with your ideal self on mental and emotional levels, and, at the same time, purposefully positioning your body in a solid, powerful stance. Remember that your physical state greatly influences your mental state - and vice versa. It's all connected: mind, body, and spirit. And if it's all connected, you have to see things as done, feel them as done, experience them as done in your body and your mind - and connect with that. In this way, you hardwire yourself for success. Some people talk about this as "tricking your mind," but I prefer to think about it as programming and conditioning the mind for the outcomes that you want.

You can prove this to yourself in a simple experiment. First, slouch down in your chair; let your shoulders sag and your head drop. In this posture, think about a large and difficult task that you need to complete at work. Notice how you feel about that task - it probably feels challenging, daunting, or even overwhelming. And your physical posture is certainly not helping you find a clear way through.

You can exacerbate this by putting your head in your hands, shaking your head and saying "no". Notice how powerful your physical posture is in determining your emotions.

Now before you get too stuck in that rather unhelpful state, we are going to snap out of it immediately. Stand up tall. Get that slouch out of your back - pull your shoulders back and down. Lift your chest out and up to the sky. Make sure both of your feet are set firmly, squarely on the ground. Breathe in a regular rhythm.

In this powerful stance, close your eyes, and focus your thinking on that work task. Decide how you are going to tackle it. See it done, and see yourself having taken the appropriate action from this powerful state. Suddenly, it feels less daunting, right? The body and mind are very connected, so work that connection to your advantage.

Executive Entrepreneur Challenge 3: Act from Your Portrait

Let's use this powerful state and carry it through to engaging with your heart to achieve your Life Well-Lived. Choose just one of the big goals you conceived in creating your portrait of a life well lived and concentrate on it. Let's work together on seeing it done. Visualize it. Be the person that has achieved that goal. Put yourself in that state where you feel and sense that it has been achieved.

Once you are there, in that space of achievement in your head and in your body, find one point on your body that you can press that's going to connect you with that single big goal. Is it your heart? Is it your forehead? Your eyebrow? Your palm? Choose one point on your body and press it to connect with that goal. In this way, you are creating a physical connection with that goal, and it's something to hang on to.

Breathe and feel and sense that goal achieved, and touch that point on your body to cement the achievement. Anytime you are feeling scattered or anxious, press this point on your body to center yourself, to find focus and grounding by reminding yourself of this bigger goal that you are on path to achieving.

The next thing I want you to do is consider the following: "Okay, if that is done, how do I behave in the next moment? What is it that I'm doing?" We have to play a little mindset trick on ourselves here to break through performance barriers:

- See it already done: step back to the other side of that door and say, "I've got to achieve this thing, I know what it feels like, I know what it feels like to be in that state, so what do I need to do now to move towards that?" Be and experience and feel that person that you know you are. Be the best version of yourself right now.

- Create momentum with one small step: do one thing right now; take action right now in that state. In this way you create momentum, which starts to move you towards bringing that vision into reality.

For example, some small actions that create momentum might include:

- Putting the date for your next holiday into your diary

- Writing the first two lines of that memo you promised to get out

- Brainstorming the key tasks that you need to complete in order to achieve a goal

- Making that first sales call of the day

This unleashes the power of momentum. Imagine a boulder at the top of the hill. It is heavy, but it contains huge amounts of energy. All it takes is leverage to get it moving. A small push or a lever that tips it forward will send the boulder crashing down the mountain. And once it is rolling, nothing will stop it until it reaches its destination. That boulder represents your potential. All you need to do to start realizing your full potential is to get moving. Use the power of momentum as leverage to get moving. Don't over-analyze things now. Just start. Or as Nike advises, "Just do it."

Add Rocket Fuel to Your Goals

I am sure you've read and heard a lot about the importance of goal setting, and many readers will already consider themselves experts in this area. But I want you to add rocket fuel, liquid propane gas (LPG), to your goals. That's the mnemonic to help you think about goal setting across three different timeframes, and it works as follows:

- Life goals – the big things you MUST do before you die

- Proximity goals – the things you must achieve in the next five years

- Graduation goals – the things you must do this year to graduate to the next stage in your growth

LPG! Rocket fuel!

I am sure you get it.

Before taking you through a couple of goal-setting exercises, I want to go back to the basics for a moment. First of all, you know that writing down your goals is absolutely key to being clear about what they are and committing yourself to them. If you have goals that are just in your head and you haven't written them down, they're not tangible - they are just in your head. There's a famous study of Yale graduates that is often quoted - you know, the one that says that the three percent of graduates who had written down their goals ended up being worth more than the ninety-seven percent who had not. Well, it turns out that study (and another similar one allegedly from Harvard graduates) was never undertaken or published. So what is the truth?

Thankfully, there is still clear evidence that writing down your goals, committing to them, and telling other people how you are doing against them makes a tremendous difference. Common sense is supported by academic studies.

For example, Gail Matthews of Dominican University in California found that over a four-week period, those who had written down their goals and committed to them publicly did significantly better at meeting them than those who simply held their goals in their heads. Further, she found that those who reported to someone else about progress against their goals did even better. So the lessons we can take from this are:

1. Write down your goals (make sure these goals engage your heart as well as your head, as we have discussed previously).

2. Make a public commitment to your goals. Tell people - your work colleagues, your family, your friends. Post your goals on the wall next to your desk at your office or next to your bedside table in your home. Publish your goals on your website, blog, or Facebook wall. Send out a tweet announcing your goals to your Twitter followers. These are all great ways to reduce your wiggle room for deciding not to try or bailing out on your goals.

3. Find someone to hold you accountable to your goals and report to that person on your progress. You can do this with a friend, a colleague, a sibling, a coach, or, as we do in our Executive Entrepreneur program, with like-minded individuals in your peer group.

Do all these three things, and your chances for success massively improve.

The key is to get committed. I learned this very early on. If you are able to see clearly in your head what you need to do, that's a crucial first step, but you must-must-MUST get committed as well, and that means taking action immediately towards something.

There are a couple of methods you can use to do this, which I outline below. Choose the method that works for best for you.

But the most important thing is that you must write your goals down so that you can see them, review them, improve them, and measure yourself against them.

Method 1: The Rocking Chair Approach

Sit down for ten to fifteen minutes for this exercise with your journal and pen. Sit down in a comfortable chair and picture yourself in a rocking chair at each of the three time points we've established in the LPG way of setting goals. Imagine yourself looking back at the period in question. From that reflective place, looking back, I want you to consider the five things that made the biggest difference. Determine what you were most proud of.

- Looking back at the age of say eighty or ninety years old, what things would you tell your friends, children, or grandchildren you were most proud of having achieved? What would you look back on and say had the greatest impact on giving you that sense of having lived a life well-lived? These are the Life goals that are most important to you, the L goals in the LPG mnemonic, and you should use these to guide your thinking on what you do in the other timeframes that we are going to consider.

- Now, pick up that rocking chair and bring it forwards in time to just five years from now. You are more proximate to today. From this position you're going to think about Proximate goals, the P in the LPG mnemonic. Looking back on those five years that you have just lived, what has created the most satisfaction in your life? What has created the most momentum towards achieving your life goals? What are you most proud of? Write down your answers. These proximate goals are incredibly important because they are achievable. Write them down. Spend some time getting familiar with them. Use them as the key ingredient, the propane, to fuel your actions in the present moment.

- Now one more time, pick up that rocking chair and bring it forward to one year from now. Put a mortarboard hat on your head and imagine yourself graduating from the next year ahead in style. Look back on the last year and celebrate in style the wins, the achievements, and the standing success that puts you in the top tier of performers. This is your focus for the year ahead, your Graduation G-level goals in the LPG mnemonic. See it done. Celebrate what you have achieved and remember that feeling. Remember that feeling and bring it forward to the present moment.

- Now stand up from that rocking chair and return to the present moment. And remember that in this present moment, you have the ability to take a few steps, a few decisions, a few actions towards your goals. It is a cliché, but it remains true: the journey of one thousand miles starts with one step. So take your first steps now. Write down your LPG goals, get more clarity, and inject some passion into the steps that you're taking now.

The beauty and the power of this approach is that it eliminates time. From all these different perspectives, we can see that our goals are connected and that the actions we take in each moment help to create our destinies. This helps to give each moment meaning, to live passionately and to act with focus as we move through our daily lives, remaining connected to the things that we value and know are important for us.

Method 2: The Brainstorm Approach

Another way into articulating your goals is through freeform brainstorming. Write down the categories or headings for the goals that are important to you. So, for example, write down and add to or adapt the following headings:

Work Goals	Personal Goals
■ Career	■ Relationships / Family
■ Current Employment / Business	■ Finances
■ Key Projects for the Year	■ Physical
	■ Emotional / Spiritual

Work through each of these areas and brainstorm out what it is you want to achieve. Spend perhaps three minutes on each category, and write down as many goals and desires as you can without determining exactly when you would achieve any of them. Just write.

Once the list is reasonably complete, go back through it and assign one of the letters, L, P, or G to the tasks, according to whether it is a Life, Proximate, or Graduation goal.

This gives you a sense of order to achieving what it is you desire. I would still encourage you to distill this list down to the top five goals in each of the three timeframes that the LPG approach uses.

Executive Entrepreneur Challenge 4: Add Rocket Fuel to Your Goals

Set aside some clear time in your schedule with no distractions to refresh or determine your goals. Use the LPG framework and either the rocking chair or brainstorming method outlined above to create a set of goals under each of the three headings:

- Lifetime goals: try to set out at least half a dozen goals that will make you happy when you look back from the age of ninety and say, "I did that!"

- Proximity goals: set at least half a dozen goals that you want to achieve in the next five years.

- Graduation goals: set no more than five goals for the next year that will move you forwards significantly towards your proximity and lifetime goals. We'll work the detail on these later in the book in Shift 3 about creating momentum. For now, I just want you to be clear about what your Graduation goals are.

Harness Pain and Pleasure

Pain and pleasure, or fear and joy, are closely linked. If you've ever jumped from a high diving board, you'll probably know this feeling. How good did it feel when you did so for the first time and managed to conquer your fear? We can use these two emotions, fear and joy, to motivate and drive us to higher levels of performance.

We can see, feel, taste, and touch achieving our ultimate goal, and we have already practiced thinking backwards from having it achieved to how we behaved. We determined the things that we did do to reach success, as well as the things we wouldn't do - and those we discarded. Now we need to add pain and pleasure to our visual imagining, associating pain with failure to achieve and pleasure with success.

One of the tricks you can do with your mindset is to consider both sides of the equation: pain and pleasure, or fear and joy. This exercise works well if you know whether you are most motivated by avoiding pain or by experiencing pleasure. We are motivated by both of these, but one of them will be dominant. Most people are hardwired to avoid pain: to survive, to not mess up, to avoid failure. They desperately want to avoid feeling these negative thoughts, and it is these drivers that motivate them to take action.

A smaller proportion of people are more motivated by moving towards experiences of pleasure, joy, and fulfillment as their primary motive. These people typically take more risks because they are not so frightened of failure.

If you're one of these kinds of people, then dwelling on sources of potential pain is not something that you find terribly helpful. Rather, you will want to see clearly all of the great experiences that you are bringing into your life.

Most people are motivated predominantly by only one of these drivers. They are either strongly driven to avoid pain ("Don't mess up," "Don't take unnecessary risks," "Don't move outside your comfort zone") or by pleasure ("Imagine what it would feel like to succeed," "How can I get that into my life?" "How amazing will that feel?")

Most people are predominantly fear avoiders rather than pleasure seekers. They will spend a lifetime avoiding messing up, rather than being prepared to make a few mistakes as they learn and grow. And this is a natural instinct: the more primitive elements of our brain direct us to stay safe from danger in what may appear as a hostile world.

And yet this is not our natural condition. We learn to walk by falling down; we learn to love by learning to forgive. My personal experience is that while it is important to harness both fear and joy, the full richness of life is experienced when we are happy and joyful. My coaching takes this approach to helping people succeed, and while I don't counsel you to ignore risks, I do encourage you to take a few well-calculated ones as you seek to learn and grow as an Executive Entrepreneur.

Executive Entrepreneur Challenge 5: Harness Pain and Pleasure in Your Goal Setting

Find a comfortable place, and sit down with your journal and a pen. Start this exercise by taking one of your key goals, ideally a Graduation G-level goal, and writing it at the top your page. Divide the page into thirds and use each third for one step in this exercise.

Step 1: Harness pleasure.

You should be familiar with this by now. I want you to close your eyes and see the goal as done. Think of all the good things that will come from this.

Write down the key things that come to your mind in the top third of the page. If it helps, use the following questions as a guide:

- How do you feel? What experiences have brought pleasure into your life? What does the success bring in terms of emotions?

- What have you achieved? How do other people view you? What does your family think about your achievement? What good things are in your life as a result of this?

- What good has come from your achievement? What is better in other people's lives as a result of your efforts? How has it made other people feel? How have you made the world a better place?

Step 2: Harness pain.

Now consider the flipside - the pain of failing to meet that achievement. On the second section of your page, write down your experiences, feelings, and emotions that would be present if you did not achieve your goal. If it helps, use the following questions to guide your thoughts:

- What have you missed out on? What did you have to give up because you did not achieve your goal? What opportunities are passing you by because you are not in the place that you need to be to take full advantage of them?

- What have you had to sacrifice? What have you had to give up because you did not achieve your goal? How does this make you feel? What do your family and friends think?

- What have you not brought into this world? Who have you failed to help? How much are you kicking yourself?

These are painful thoughts. Capture them and use them as a driver to take action and as a reminder when you feel like procrastinating. Notice that we are harnessing fear to get us moving here, rather than using fear to make the task bigger than it seems.

Step 3: Create momentum.

The third and final step in this exercise is to get moving. Look back at the pain or fear factors, and remind yourself of all the good things that you will achieve when you succeed. Use these as reminders and motivators to encourage you to take action both now and in the future.

Now in the final third of the page, write down the key actions that you need to take in order to achieve your goal. It doesn't matter whether they are big or small, just write them down and get clarity on what needs to happen. Use the following as a prompt if it helps:

- Whom do I need to speak to? Which other people can help me achieve my goal and how can I best engage them?

- What resources do I need to achieve my goal? How am I going to acquire these and make best use of them?

- What other key chunks of work do I need to complete in order to achieve my goal? Is there an order to these? What small steps can I take to create momentum in each of these areas?

Review this list, and select one or two actions that you can take in the next five minutes. Now, put away your pen and paper, and do those one or two actions. Don't think any more. Just do them.

Use your mind and find some pain points in there to provoke and motivate yourself to act. Dwelling on the pain of failure can serve as the grit in your shoe that makes you uncomfortable and forces you to take action towards your goal, each and every day.

Small daily steps in the right direction add up to big achievements over time. This is how wars are won, how businesses are built, and how you can transform your career.

If you're clear about your goal, you have grit in your shoe. You use that grit to take small, daily steps toward your goal. Say you make five steps toward your goal, each and every day, just small, tiny baby steps. Well, that's 35 steps each week, 140 steps each month, 1,820 steps each year, etc.

Tiny steps that you walk (enact) on a daily basis will amount to great things. As you take these smaller steps, over time you can look back and find you've moved great distances. You will be able to look back each month and notice how far you've moved. That's how the outstanding performance of the successful Executive Entrepreneur is built.

Fight over Flight

When you're attacking a problem or a big challenge, as I'm sure you know, there are two main responses. The first is flight - curling up and saying, "Oh, I'll let someone else handle that," "I'll do that tomorrow," or "Maybe, I need to think about that further . . ."

The other response is fight, as in, "I'm going to get right on this," "No time like the present," or "I'm going to kill this task, knock it out right away."

Both fight and flight are survival instincts. What we want to achieve in our mindset is the absolute presence of mind that comes with being in flow, being in the moment and moving forwards. And one of the questions we've been grappling with is - how do you trigger that state of flow? How do you get into that zone where nothing else is present - no fears, troubles, memories from the past, or items on today's to-do list - nothing except the task at hand?

Here's the insight that I want to share with you. We certainly don't get into that zone through flight. If we run away from our problems, if we curl up or decide to deal with them later, there's no momentum to carry us forward. But we can achieve that state of flow through the fight reaction; it's one of the first visceral responses.

So if your reaction is to fight, that's great. You are using fear and potential pain to motivate yourself into action. And as Tony Robbins urges, "Get uncomfortable; use that position of discomfort and fear to make a shift." But don't stay in that state; simply use it to get into motion. And as soon as you're in motion, tackling the problem, you end up releasing the fear because in getting into motion, you start to figure out where you're going and what you need to achieve to see it done. All you're doing is taking action to bring your goal into reality.

On a very personal level, sometimes I wake up knowing that I'm just not "in the zone." I feel low, I feel down, and I want just another half-hour in bed.

This is the battle of "mind over mattress," a phrase I picked up from Robin Sharma. This is one of the times that we need to both dig into our willpower and exercise the discipline of establishing good habits. Brushing our teeth is a good habit, right? So is getting out of bed early to start our day well. I remind myself of this, and take one small action to build momentum. I throw off the duvet. That's all. One simple, small action kicks in the habit of my morning routine.

I get up, I get into my personal workout area, I stretch and breathe, I give thanks for the day ahead, and I work out gently, whether with some simple stretches or more vigorous, depending on my fitness plan.

And if you still find yourself procrastinating, find ways to remove all obstacles that make it hard to get momentum. For example, if putting your running kit on in the morning makes you feel bad, put it on the night before. Think how good you will feel after that run or workout; program your brain to remember that elated feeling you experienced the last time you did exercise, and commit in advance to feeling that again. Then, immediately when you wake - don't think - instead, simply put on your shoes, get out that door, walk around the block, go for a run, breathe the air, and get into motion - use that motion to excise all those toxins, those fear hormones, those chemicals running around your body - get rid of them, breathe them out, and move in motion so that you're literally moving into that state where things are possible.

Keep a Journal

Benjamin Franklin started each day by posing to himself the question, "What good will I do today?" and then meditated on it in his journal. When you meditate on your day's agenda and journal about it, you create clarity about what needs to get done. If you tie this into reviewing and reflecting on your goals for the year or beyond, you create momentum. The habit of journaling, therefore, needs to be a daily one. Like brushing your teeth.

And like brushing your teeth, you'll find that you feel much better when you do it. If you forget or fail to do it, your day or weeks start to get a bit more scrappy and unfocused. To extend the metaphor of brushing your teeth: "Your breath starts to smell." I know that's vivid, but hopefully it will encourage you to start journaling if you don't already do so.

It is also a great way to reflect on how to get things done: a space in which you can work through what needs to happen in order for a major achievement to be reached; a place where you can set down your thoughts on something for later review.

Start your day not only by thinking about what you need to do, but also about whom you need to work with to achieve it. By reflecting on how you work with other people and your wider organization, and by recording this in your journal, you will find success. In the book Long Walk to Freedom, Nelson Mandela made this point very beautifully. He realized that he alone could not change things: one person alone is powerless, but put an organization around that person and he or she can achieve great things. And Mandela did that, so powerfully, changing not only South Africa but also the world. So think about who you need to help you along the way and reach out to them.

For example, recently during my journaling time, I found myself meditating on a major goal: a client task that I had to do involving a big program, running across five different countries with multiple projects in each country and multiple strands within each project.

I needed to work out the links between the various strands. I sat with my journal and proceeded to break it down into four main areas of work, each with a key outcome that needed to be accomplished. From this, I was able to quickly identify the tasks that I needed to do or commission others to do. From a daunting task, I was able to gain clarity and momentum.

Of course, I could have done this using a sheet of paper from the photocopier. But these get discarded, and the physical act of writing down your thoughts in a journal for review later is an incredibly powerful one. It helps you get clarity, avoid procrastination, and stop feeling overwhelmed - things that can stop most people from taking action. By breaking it down, visualizing and chunking your work, you can simplify a complex task. You play around with it to make it clear, sequential, and manageable, all the while recording your actions.

As a way of helping you here, at a very personal level, I want to give you an insight into how I journal. I've developed this approach by combining the best elements of many great coaches and entrepreneurs, from Benjamin Franklin through to modern day coaches, such as Robin Sharma and Brendan Burchard. Just as I have developed my own approach, I encourage you to find what works best for you. Feel free to adopt this framework and adapt it to your own needs and practices.

Every day, in the morning before the day starts, I sit down with two fresh pages of my journal. Here is what it looks like in outline:

Diagram 3: Daily Journal Outline

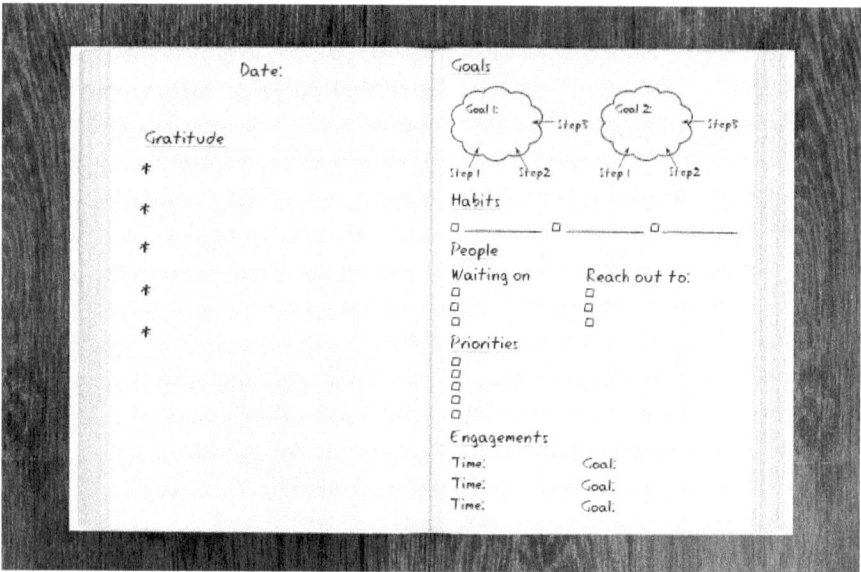

On the left, I write down my gratitudes: no matter how challenging the day ahead, I start by being grateful for all that I have and all the opportunity that awaits. In this frame of mind, the day looks more productive, and negativity cannot encroach and pull me down.

Then on the right hand side, I set out the following:

- **Goals:** I physically write out my top two to five goals that I am working on and what I need to do over the next few weeks or months to achieve those goals.

- **Habits:** I write down the three habits that I am seeking to make routine and part of my conscious practice, much as Benjamin Franklin used to cycle through habits he wanted to install in his daily practice.

- **People:** I write down whom I am waiting to hear from and whom I need to reach out to. The people I am waiting to hear from are those that I look for when I open my email system.

I only look for these people, and then I reach out to them if I have not heard from them and write quick emails to the others on my "reach out to" list.

- **Priorities:** I write down my top three to five priorities for the day, things that I must achieve. This is not the same as a detailed to-do list - I just stick to the top priorities that I want to work on, get done, and shift forwards - such as drafting a chapter of my next book or making my five daily networking calls. I may add other tasks, both personal and work oriented, to my list of things to do, but I make sure to mark out the top three to five things that I will move heaven and earth to achieve, and I make sure I start the day by getting one of them done first (eat that frog!).

- **Diary:** I note key meetings coming up in the day and set my objectives for those meetings so that I know what I want to get out of them. If I don't have a clear objective, I seriously question whether I should ditch or delegate the meeting to someone else.

Two small quirks that I'll share: I write the bullet points for gratitude starting with a "+" symbol, and I write each habit, each person I need to hear from or speak to, and each priority with a square box in front, and I place a V for "victory" when I have completed that item.

Executive Entrepreneur Challenge 6: Establish (or Refine) Your Journaling

If you don't already have a journal, then get one. Ideally it should have clean, blank pages that you can write and draw freeform in, without the constraint of lines. I personally love the beautiful Moleskin journals. It's worth spending that little bit of extra money on your journal to make it special because it will be a powerful aid in your drive to achieve your goals.

I remember Jim Rohn said that his kids used to joke with him, asking, "Dad, why have you got a twenty-dollar book with nothing in it?" He would laugh, replying, "This book is worth more than any other book that I've owned. It's got so much that is priceless within it."

Once you've got your journal with pristine, clean pages, for the next thirty days, I want you to do the following each day:

- Record the things in your life that you're grateful for.

- Write down your Graduation, G-level goals for the year and the key things you need to do to achieve them. Yes, it's repetition - but as Tony Robbins points out, "Repetition is the mother of skill." I want you to ingrain those goals so deeply into your brain that you cannot fail but to focus on achieving them each and every day.

- Reflect on who's going to help you achieve those big goals. Whom do you need to reach out to help you achieve each big goal and whom are you waiting on?

- Revisit your agenda for the day at hand - ideally this should be one that you decided and wrote out for yourself the evening before (see more about this later in the book).

- Spend some time considering the tasks for the day and highlight those in particular that move you towards your Graduation goals for the year. What will you do to move each forward?

This should become a daily habit - looking back on what you accomplished the previous day, what you determined to be the most important three to five tasks for the day at hand, and meditating on them.

Chapter 3 - Skillset

The first shift we covered under the chapter on mindset looked at engaging your heart and making sure that you follow your passion in life. Do what you love and the temptation is to think that the rest will fall into place. But, sadly, that is not true. You still have to have systems and ways of working that enable you to achieve results, and this chapter explores two of the fundamental skillsets that you will need to develop and continue to improve as you build your career. These two shifts are about getting strategic in what you focus on; and then making sure that you create the momentum you need to turn strategy into action.

Shift 2: Get Strategic

Great strategy helps you achieve your goals. Bad strategy gets in the way, clutters, and confuses. But it all starts with having a clear goal to achieve and being committed to doing so. Spend a moment before working through this chapter to review your LPG goals. The previous chapter should help with that if you've not already work through the exercises there.

And as you read this chapter, use one or more of those goals in the exercises that follow. It doesn't matter whether your goal is to increase your financial reward, gain promotion, execute flawlessly on a key project, or any other goal that you may have set for yourself. What I set out below, if followed, will give you a clear strategy for helping you achieve those goals.

So many books have been written on strategy that it can be hard to filter out the good from the bad and the ugly. My job is not to write another book on the subject. You can get plenty of those right off the bookshelf. I want to keep things very simple here so that theory doesn't bamboozle you.

I also want you to recognize that this shift, of getting strategic, is one that even great executives struggle with. So you are not alone if this feels hard to you. One of the main reasons it is a difficult shift to make (and to write about) is that developing great strategy is not a one-size-fits-all process. People often fall back on what they know has worked in the past, expecting it to work by default in the future. Our tendency is to work on things that are easy to change or to use approaches and tools that we are comfortable with, or both.

But, as the saying goes, "If all you have is a hammer, everything looks like a nail." And developing great strategy that really creates focus and drive is one that requires a great deal of flexibility, insight, and imagination. You can't just pull out the hammer and start hammering.

You've got to think very carefully and deeply about the challenges you face and your options for tackling them. You must test your understanding rigorously as you shape your strategy. And you must think clearly about who can help you achieve your goals and how you focus your effort, energy, and attention to crack the challenges that are going to mark your performance out above that of your competitors.

Many executives find themselves most busy putting out fires, tackling a problem here and there, running from meeting to meeting, and generally doing good work. If this sounds like you, then in essence what that means is that you are letting other people set your goals for you. You have accepted, and may even feel happy about, the fact that you are busy being busy. But you're not setting your own goals and your own agenda. You're not being sufficiently strategic, taking a step back and looking at the challenges that you face, the projects that you take on, and how you allocate your time and resources - not just you - to those problems.

It's in the second shift that the real transformation begins. I've been surprised over the years how many executives really do struggle with some of the challenges that getting strategic means. Let's be honest here. If you're not getting promoted farther in your organization or if you're recently promoted and thinking, "My goodness, how am I going to make the best of this opportunity that I've got there?" then you've got to start facing up to the challenges and getting strategic. I often find that when executives struggle with this, it's usually because there are one or more hidden flaws in how they're tackling problems.

Creating momentum rests on being clear about your goal and having some ideas about the best way to achieve it. This is the essence of strategy. You may not have everything right, and that's fine. But it is important to be clear about your goal and strategy, even if you move through these stages quickly, before moving onto creating momentum. If you're not clear where you're going and how to get there, then any road will do.

A really good example of this occurred during the credit crunch when many banks lost sight of the big picture and focused on short-term profit rather than long-term sustainability. People lost sight of the detail and failed to understand the overall strategic challenge. They, therefore, failed to pick an appropriate strategic direction in the circumstances. Only a very few people remarked, "Hey, we need to understand this business model properly. If we don't understand this business model, then we don't know that we're investing wisely." A few people saw the big picture and selected the appropriate strategic response. They placed bets against what the main banks were doing and made billions while banks went under and governments stepped in to prop them up. I am sure you know the story. So spend time on the strategy and understand it well. Once you've got that nailed, then you can start to look at how you create momentum.

A Strategic Mindset

While I have included this section on strategy as a skill that you can learn, it is important that you adopt the right mindset. There are four key parts to adopting a strategic mindset:

- **Be inquisitive:** you need to ask questions, and you need to know when you've not quite found the answers. Those questions aren't necessarily difficult to ask, but they should be searching and get to the heart of the matter.

- **Take an outsider's perspective:** you need to think about how you explain your thinking to an outsider. If you can't explain it clearly, you probably don't understand it well enough to be certain that you have a rock-solid strategy. And if you can explain it clearly, you are much better placed to determine whether it holds water.

- **Listening to instincts**: this does not mean acting without thought or shooting from the hip. It means knowing when you've not yet managed to get the full clarity you need to act, or alternatively, knowing when you have enough information to act.

- **Keep it real:** a strategy that sits on the shelf or a website looking pretty is no good to anyone. It's got to drive action. We deal with that in the next shift, but let's stay focused on developing the strategy for now, knowing that it has to drive action or it will be useless.

Case Study: Starbucks

Howard Schultz established a global company and brand in Starbucks in an incredibly short space of time, thanks in large measure to the clarity and simplicity of his strategy for creating and then dominating his market. As a younger man, he was working at a company also called Starbucks, which sold coffee. When Schultz visited Italy, he saw an amazing café culture there where people were standing around, chatting with the barista, watching the barista doing his job, and to Schultz it seemed an almost magical experience in terms of enjoying an espresso. If we recall the Scan-Focus-Act model, we could say that Schultz found himself scanning during his trip to Italy.

Schultz knew that there was a need in American consumerism that wasn't currently being met. He sensed an opportunity. He didn't know for a fact, but he sensed an opportunity - that he could create something within America that would be truly unique there. So he continued scanning, looking at different possibilities, and finally he brought a proposal back to his company. When he told them what he wanted to do, they weren't sure - so he went ahead and did it anyway. He set up his own coffee place called Il Giorno.

In Il Giorno, he worked out many of the kinks in what it meant to serve great coffee to Americans (read as Schultz's Focus phase). Schultz worked out that what Americans wanted really wasn't the strong espresso. They wanted different flavors and a more milky, but still great, coffee. Also they wanted an environment where they could sit and catch up easily with friends, but they also wanted the option for takeaway, coffees to go. Schultz worked out much of his business model - his strategy - just by doing it quickly, a very fast iteration in the grand scheme of things from the Starbucks' perspective.

By scanning and focusing, he achieved very quickly a proven little model, and when he returned to Starbucks the second time, he presented them not only with a proposal, but a proposal couched in a burning platform for change - so they accepted it, buying Il Giorno and Schultz's model.

Schultz, who'd already been tirelessly chasing his dreams, then took off running (read as Schultz's Act phase) - delivering a massive explosion of cafés and coffee houses in America that made Starbucks into a truly global brand.

The first thing I'd like you to note from this story is that Schultz took action. A strategy is not about talk, it is about action. And unless the strategy drives action, it's useless.

The second thing to note is that Schultz's strategy was clear: he wanted to set up an American chain of coffee houses that promoted a café culture. He was very concrete in his goal. And it was based on a clear need, albeit he didn't necessarily have the empirical evidence for that when he set it up. He, from his gut, felt that there was a clear need for the café culture to be brought to America - so he acted.

Schulz also had a coherent plan of action: he set up a proof of concepts coffee house to prove how the café culture and service could be brought to the States, learned from the challenges he faced in doing so, and then scaled it. So there was a clear understanding of the problem, the diagnosis, and from there he had a clear guiding policy to drive through what the implementation of that meant. Then he had coherent action behind it that drove his business forwards. This is the essence of good strategy.

Common Flaws in Developing Strategy

Let's look at two common pitfalls in developing strategy. The first is failing to get absolute clarity and insight into how to solve big corporate challenges. If you're not sufficiently clear, then you're going to come unstuck. I've been surprised at how many executives walk into meetings thinking that they're prepared and then as soon as an executive around the table asks them a question, things start to fold, the cracks start to appear, and they think, "Oh my goodness, I haven't really thought that one through yet."

Make sure that you're clear about how to solve those corporate challenges. There are lots of tools that I could share with you. We don't have the time or space in this book to go through all of them, but I will just share one key insight with you: even the big-strategy consulting firms frequently get strategy wrong! Organizations will pay lots of money to bring a big consultancy firm in to look at the problems in the organization.

The consultancy will ask people what's happening and then write a nice report, and one of two things will happen. Either it will sit on a shelf and won't get implemented, or alternatively, it will get implemented and result in confusion and chaos. Now often there's a better outcome than either of those, but those two things can typically happen. I've seen it many, many times, and I am sure you'll have your own war stories on this front, either from firsthand experience or amongst your peer set.

The reason that those two patterns happen is because the consulting firm has not really understood the organization properly. They'll hide behind phrases like "the strategy was poorly executed," or they will try to sell further project delivery consulting teams in behind the strategy to sort out the confusion and chaos that they created. But it need not go like this.

It is worth repeating: the reason these patterns happen is because the consultancy firm has not really understood the organization they are consulting into and the full extent of the challenges it faces. Well, guess what? You do understand your organization and the challenges you face. So my argument is that you and the colleagues around you are best placed to make the shifts, to set your own agenda, and to drive for the changes you need to make them real. That is how I coach the executives I work with. Sure, you might need a bit of extra mentoring, coaching, or support - but your strategy must be based on your own agenda and your understanding of what is likely to work. You are best placed to give the strategic insight and to be able to shift the organization forward. But you do have to apply yourself using simple and powerful tools, some of which I share with you right here in this book.

The second challenge that people face in developing and implementing strategy is that they don't have the ability to inspire people. Part of the reason they don't manage to inspire people is often because they're not sufficiently clear about the challenge or the solution. They don't have sufficient clarity about what their strategy is and they therefore find it hard to engage with their audience and give them confidence that their leader has a firm grip on things.

Components of Good Strategy

The word "strategy" can often be misinterpreted or made confusing. But at its core, every good strategy has four key elements, the first three of which Richard Rumelt noted in his book Good Strategy Bad Strategy:

- A clear diagnosis of the problem based on a deep understanding of the current situation and the opportunities and challenges you are tackling

- A theme or principle that frames the strategy, adds clarity, and sets the direction of travel (something Rumelt calls a "guiding policy")

- A coherent set of actions (ideally comprehensive and mutually exclusive) that give focus and drive to the direction of travel. Strategy without action is useless, and good strategy will make clear what needs to happen and in what order.

To these three elements that Rumelt expands on in his book, I add a fourth to keep people focused:

- A clear goal or outcome in mind, that is achievable even if the apparent odds seem stacked against it

One key distinction to make is that a strategy, while it needs to frame a coherent set of actions, is not the same as business planning. I've seen many strategies that fail to give clarity and direction because they end up essentially as high-level project plans. While there may be a semblance of order, they fail to ignite people and bring clarity and insight as to why the tasks are required.

One way of avoiding getting bogged down in the detail of planning when you are developing your strategy is to ask whether you are answering a "what" or a "who" question. If it is a "what" question and you answer it by clarifying what needs to be done, then it is more likely to be strategic. If it is a "who" question and you are clarifying who will take the action, then it is more likely to be in the business and project planning arena. That's not to say the actions are wrong. Just put them in a different document and don't try to paint them up as a strategy.

Great strategies also have two key qualities. They are both:

- **Clear and direct**: they use simple language and speak clearly to the average person. If you can't understand an organization's strategy at first read, then the chances are that it is lacking this quality. It is difficult to understate how important simplicity and directness are in terms of writing down and communicating your strategy. If the people reading or hearing about your strategy do not understand it, then it's not much use to them. And if they are your employees, then is not much use to you either. So read your strategy, give it to people across your organization, and ask them what they think about its clarity and directness. If you're not happy with the responses, then this is a signal that you need to do something to improve your strategy.

- **Achievable**: in the world of strategy we call this "proximity." Great strategies, while seeming bold and audacious, are also achievable. Big, hairy, audacious goals are no use if they are not achievable. They just switch people off. If people don't believe something is achievable, then why would they put any effort or passion into achieving it? So look carefully at your strategy and the goals that your strategy is seeking to achieve, and make sure that they pass this test. That they have proximity. For proximity is power, both in networking and in strategy.

Developing Clarity

One of a leader's key roles is to set a clear strategy that can be explained, understood, and acted upon. To do this you need to ensure you have a good understanding of the strategic challenges you are facing and how to tackle these. Once your strategy is clear and understood, it's going to be much easier to set the goals for your organization or business unit, and people are going to be much clearer about what they need to do and how they fit into the bigger strategic picture. This is a shift that all leaders have to make. You've got to move from having others define your goals to taking control and announcing, "This is what's going to happen."

Now that's not to say that setting good strategy is easy. It's often not easy, and there's a lot of fuzzy thinking around it. That's because people struggle with being very clear about exactly what needs to change and how to make those changes happen.

If your strategy documents don't answer the key questions about what needs to change and how the team is going to make it happen, then you're not giving insight. So many strategic statements fail to do this. Richard Rumelt gives a lovely example of an internal bank memo to staff that read, "Our primary strategy is one of customer-focused intermediation." Well, it might sound impressive to some ears, but it doesn't mean very much. Customer-focused intermediation? Intermediation is lending and borrowing. "Customer-focused" means that they focus on their customers. So what they focus on doing is lending and borrowing to their customers. They are a bank... Surprise!

Don't dress your strategy up in fluff. Make sure that you're very clear about exactly what needs to change and what needs to happen. If you've got a problem, a strategic problem, then remember this:

recognizing that problem is not the same as being very clear about how to solve it. You've got to really understand and get clear on what needs to change and how to make those changes happen.

How do you get unstuck? Einstein stated, "If you can't explain it clearly, you don't understand it well enough." You've got to understand your problems. So many executives I see struggle with really getting down to the heart of the matter and finding the two, three, or four really key changes that will make a shift happen. They get busy being busy. They fire off a dozen memos, declaring, "We've got to do this, this, this," but you've got to narrow it down and spend some time getting clear about the strategic problems that you've got to shift.

The best way I know how to do that is to take an outsider's perspective to the problem. If you can't explain it to an outsider, you probably don't understand it well enough. Don't get caught up in all the technical detail. Think about being an outsider detective or consultant, and ask simple questions.

It's really important to be simple and ask simple questions because they're powerful and hard to flannel. Steve Jobs did this brilliantly. He didn't dress things up in all sorts of fancy corporate flannel. He got down to hard talks and asked very simple, direct, straight questions.

Once you get the answers to those questions, then you've got to boil it down, to consolidate and clarify. Try to reduce things down to those three or four key changes that you need to implement to deliver your vision and goals.

A very good way of checking your understanding is to summarize what you have heard in your own words. As you reflect back, you'll either find a gap or an additional area that needs to be discussed, or you'll be moving the conversation on nicely to the next stage. Either way, it's a great tool to ensure you keep the discussion moving in the right direction.

A good metaphor for getting clear is to imagine going to a specialist doctor - let's say a cancer specialist - because the problem you are presenting could be caused by a cancer - say a lump in your breast or that you're up every night going to urinate frequently.

You fear something may be wrong, so you're taking the brave step of presenting yourself to the doctor with those symptoms to find out more, probably because you want to get rid of your fear as well as the symptoms.

I've used this serious example of visiting a cancer specialist with caution and for two reasons. Firstly, in and of itself, I hope it is helpful for some people facing such fears. But this book is about business, and in work as well as life, you also need to tackle big, strategic challenges that, if handled well, will enable you to fix and grow your business. So strategic decisions can be momentous for your business, and you need to treat them with equal care.

When you go to the specialist doctor with these symptoms, if she's on top of her game, she'll listen carefully to why you've come, listen to your symptoms, do a physical examination, and draw some initial conclusions. And if there is a risk that something serious is wrong, she won't just send you off with some antibiotics; she'll take the time to get more tests so that she can be very clear what the problem is. Most times the results will come back showing the problem is benign, and you don't need to worry. She knows that. She may even tell you that to put your mind at rest while the tests are being processed, but she does not want to take any risk with your life, so she gets the tests done. She makes sure she has all the information she needs before she gives you a diagnosis. And when she does, she'll give you that diagnosis in terms that you understand. And remember a clear diagnosis is element one in developing great strategy.

Now if it is bad news and you do have some form of cancer, she won't leave things there. The next step is to decide on a course of action. But with cancer treatments, it is often not so clear what that course of action is. There are many different treatment options (surgery, chemotherapy, radiation treatment, hormone therapy, and active surveillance - to name a few), and it can be bewildering and confusing to know which option is right for you. Each of those treatments has different side effects and consequences.

So she'll work carefully through the options with you and help you decide on the best course of treatment, looking at the pros and cons of each and helping you reach the right decision for you and your family. And that treatment route is your "guiding theme" or "policy" - i.e., element two, the second key ingredient of good strategy.

But there is more to do now. You and the medical team around you need to take action. You need to act firmly, decisively, and in a coordinated way to ensure that the right things happen in the right order to give you the best chance of conquering the cancer and living as well as possible through this difficult time. So the doctor will sit down with you and explain the course of action, and you'll work out what adjustments you need to make to fit that course of treatment into your life. This is the third element of great strategy in business, where you set out a clear and coherent course of action with clear steps along the way that enable you to know you are making progress and that you review and adjust if you are not. You need to be able to fit this course of action into the daily work of your business. If you don't, the chances are you're not going to fix the problems you're trying to fix. As we are talking about life and death here, I doubt you'll shy away from making that course of action clear.

Finally, if you look at the two qualities of great strategy again - clarity and proximity - you will notice that the doctor applies those same qualities to her work. If she's a good doctor, then she won't dress up her interaction with you in fluffy medical terms that you don't understand. She'll take the time to explain it clearly in plain English, even if some of the issues are complex and the decisions are finely balanced. If you can't understand it, she should take her time to ensure that you understand the issues rather than just insisting, "Do this. Trust me."

Be Innovative

A large proportion of what great leaders do is routine: habits of behavior that would not distinguish them from us. For example, Mandela used to clear his mind and get his body going for the day ahead as the President of South Africa by walking and thinking. Richard Branson spends a lot of time in short, sharp, focused conversations with people, reviewing progress on his various enterprises. Steve Jobs used to bring his top team together once a week to discuss ideas and progress on initiatives running across the company. These simple routines are second nature and habit, and certainly things that we can adopt too.

What distinguishes these people is how they use their routines to generate insight. They are constantly scanning their thoughts and conversations for opportunities to make a difference. They look for the unexpected connections, the flashes of insight that put them way out ahead of the competition. Steve Jobs, for example, when he visited Toshiba, found an extraordinarily small hard drive, which Toshiba was wondering what to do with. He quickly snapped up an exclusive deal with them and brought out the iPod. So much else flowed from there.

So how can we be more innovative? There are four interlocking ways that you can use to develop this skill in your own practice:

- ***Be outstanding at one thing and leverage that:*** to be innovative we have to be outstanding in what we do. Innovating on top of something average creates something a bit better than average. Innovating on top of something that is already world-class creates an unbeatable strategic position. Jobs demonstrated this with brilliance in bringing out the iPod, which built upon Apple's brand and reputation for insanely great and really cool products. Apple was not only iconic, but it was truly great at combining software and hardware. Jobs knew this and leveraged it to great effect as he innovated in the marketplace.

- **Let it brew:** sometimes the best way to find an answer to a problem is to let it brew. The philosopher and mathematician Bertrand Russell demonstrated this perfectly as a method of solving tough problems. When unable to answer a specific problem, he wrote in the *Conquest of Happiness,*
I have found... the best plan is to think about it with very great intensity - the greatest intensity of which I am capable - for a few hours or days, and at the end of that time give orders, so to speak, that the work is to proceed underground. After some months I return consciously to the topic and find that the work has been done.

  Jobs too let it brew before bringing out the iPod: he had in mind the device but had not yet seen the technology, so he was scanning the horizon to find it. He let the problem brew until he found the solution.

- **Be opportunistic:** Sometimes opportunity presents itself, and we must seize the moment. The key to this form of innovation is being open. The solution may not come immediately, but to the patient person doors usually open.

  I found this in my own earlier career as a young civil servant, trying to reduce the burden on schools of reading and responding to the various dictates issued from the Department of Education. My own idea was to leverage the power of this newfangled thing called the Internet. At the time, the department had only just started to develop its web-based services. I wanted to create an A-Z of school leadership and management that would replace the need to issue hardcopy documentation every time a policy changed and expected the school to remember that something had changed either recently or in more distant memory. The idea was simple: write short web-based articles on each key topic that a school leader or manager needs to deal with and link to other key documentation from this.

The articles could be updated quickly and easily as policy changed, and we could alert school leaders and managers to any significant changes. The idea was too newfangled for the department, and I failed to get funding initially. However, when a minister for the Department of Education said that he wanted to tackle the problem by issuing a complete set of documentation to every school in hardcopy, three-ring binders, the director in charge of this area of work began to tear his hair out. Though I was only a junior civil servant at the time, I happened to be in the right meeting where the senior civil servant was outlining his problem. I was able to seize the opportunity to get my idea surfaced at the right level within the organization and the idea was funded. It stayed on the top-ten most popular pages for the department for several years to follow until a different service replaced it.

My advice now to people I coach is to be open to opportunities, wherever they arise - whether from a visit to a manufacturer (such as Jobs' visit to Toshiba) or a conversation with your peers and juniors (as in my own example above).

- **Combine two or more ingredients:** by putting two or more ingredients together, it is possible to find new solutions. We can do this with people, by bringing together different minds to solve a problem. We can do with technology, as Jobs did when he saw the mini hard drive that Toshiba created and combined it with his idea for having music in your pocket (which was not a new idea at the time). And it can be done with process improvement, where you look for the root cause of the problem and by tackling that, create multiple opportunities for innovation and improvement.

Case Study: Oprah Winfrey

Oprah Winfrey is one of the most successful and powerful women in media. Her outstanding skill was and remains her ability to draw out great and authentic stories from people and drive at the human truth at the heart of challenging issues.

While in her early 20s she carved out a successful talk show career, it was in her early 30s (during the mid-1980s) that her success was truly founded with the Oprah Winfrey Show. It was this foundation of being truly world-class at one thing that allowed Oprah to innovate later in her career.

She founded Harpo Productions ("Oprah" spelt backwards) in 1988, a decade later co-founded Oxygen Media, a company dedicated to producing media programs for women, and now the Oprah Winfrey Network. While the programming may not be innovative, her grasp of the media industry and her ability to bring ideas from conception into reality is, I would argue, a powerful example of leveraging world-class position to innovate in business.

And she has not only forced innovation and change in her industry, but also the country at large. The "Oprah Bill," signed by Bill Clinton, created the first American-wide database of convicted child abusers. In 1998 she was named one of Time Magazine's 100 Most Influential People of the 20th century.

Case Study: Wade's Water

One feature of great strategy is the element of surprise or innovation, which to many seems obvious but only when explained: the leader is able to see something that others do not and takes advantage of this.

A friend of mine, Wade, runs a very successful water company with an unusual business model. Essentially his business model is to show people and businesses that they pay a lot for the water that they are using. From here, Wade shows them that his solution would allow them to pay less. What Wade's company does is recycle and clean water. They put in place the equipment, which they maintain, and the client (people and businesses) pays a lease on the equipment.

Wade's company sold its first services in the UK by using a fantastically simple and strategic marketing process that Wade called "chimney-stacking."

They figured out which businesses would be interested in their service by literally driving around to where the industrial areas were and searching for chimneys. Then they would approach the companies in the area and ask, "Do you want to cut your costs?" And nine times out of ten, the answer was - "Sure, tell me more . . ." How elegantly simple and powerful is that?

Wade found his business model so strong he wanted to extend it farther. So he decided to chimney stack on a global scale. He looked around and asked, "Where are the biggest opportunities for me to take this business model?" He scanned the world and focused on how he was going to make his business model work more broadly, diagnosing potential problems and where the biggest opportunities lay. As a result of this process, he chose the Middle East where there were massive building and industrial development programs going on. With this decision taken, he acted positively, moving his family and building the business contacts and infrastructure needed to generate a scalable and powerful business that continues to go from strength to strength.

Executive Entrepreneur Challenge 7: Look for Innovation

Use a fresh set of pages in your journal or use the template in the workbook for this exercise. Identify one key challenge you are tackling at work on which you would like to innovate, and write this down at the top of the page.

Step 1: Scan using the four approaches to innovation outlined above.

Write down a few ideas on how you can innovate on the challenge you are working on, using each of the four methods outlined above. You can use the following questions as prompts if it helps:

- Be outstanding at one thing and leverage that:
    - How can you build on your strengths in what you are great at as you seek to innovate in this area of challenge?
    - What previous innovations have you introduced that you can learn from?

- o Who in your organization is outstanding in this area? And how can you involve them in this problem solving?

- Let it brew:

  - o Is this something that you can leave for a little while?

  - o What do you need to think about now so that you can reassure yourself that you have thought deeply and clearly about the problem before putting it away to gestate?

- Be opportunistic:

  - o What situations can you create or put yourself in so that you might have the chance to be more opportunistic about tackling the challenge?

  - o What else is going on within your organization that is relevant, that you can use to help yourself to be more creative and find solutions to your problems?

- Combine two or more ingredients:

  - o What other problems can you combine with this one to help force a more creative solution?

  - o Which other parts of your organization can you share this challenge with to help yourself to innovate?

Step 2: Focus on one or two ideas that you have identified.

Review this long list of ideas and sources of inspiration, and take a few moments to write down your thoughts as you reflect and bring focus to what you need to do in order to be more innovative. If it helps, use the following questions as prompts:

- Do any of the ideas you have written down yield insights for you now?

- Which of the ideas look most promising as lines of enquiry to pursue?

Step 3: Take action.

Once again, review your reflections from the second step, and identify actions that you can take today that will help you move towards a more innovative and creative solution to your problem.

Try to take one of these actions as soon as you finish this exercise. For the others, make sure you set aside time in your diary to make them happen.

Ensuring Proximity

Let's stick with the doctor metaphor and how doctors tackle the bombshell of handling a cancer diagnosis. One of the first questions the patient is going to ask is "What's the likelihood I am going to get better, doc?" How doctors respond to that question is one of the toughest parts of their role because everybody is different and every case is different. Miracles happen, but statistics also play out too. So the doctor may give you hope by sharing stories and examples of people who have been cured. And cures and breakthroughs are made all the time.

A different example that I love and use often occurred when Kennedy told America in 1961 that the US would put a man on the moon by the end of the 1960s. To many this seemed incredible and at face value, one might say it lacked proximity. Was it really achievable?

But the announcement was based on sound analysis of the technologies available to the United States and how American scientists could exploit these to leap ahead of Russia in the space race. In particular, the heavy thrust rocket technology the United States had begun to develop was years ahead of the Russians, and they knew that it would take a long time for the Russians to be able to catch up and replicate that technology. So they set a goal of putting a man on the moon, knowing that to achieve it would require full use and development of their cutting-edge technology.

By changing the rules of the game, the Americans were able to leapfrog the Russians in the space age. They also leveraged their investments in talented scientists and engineers to great effect as they made the other breakthroughs needed to achieve the goal. So what seemed like an incredible claim did actually pass the test of proximity: it was achievable with the right investment. And we know history proved Kennedy right.

Executive Entrepreneur Challenge 8: Develop a Transformation Map

A great tool that gives line of sight to your strategic objective and enables you to test proximity and share your thinking with others is a tool called a "transformation map." In this challenge, I walk you through how to produce one.

To complete the exercise, I want you to take one specific goal that you have set for yourself or your organization, and use this in the following three exercises. Work through each step in sequence, and allow yourself anywhere between one hour and a day to complete these exercises, depending on the scale and complexity of the goal and the challenges you face in achieving it.

The output is going to fit on one piece of A4 paper in a format called a "transformation map." This will give you an incredibly powerful tool for explaining to others and reminding yourself about what needs to happen.

Step 1: Scan the horizon.

In this first stage of opening out your strategy, I want you to think broadly about what's going on. In this Scan phase, you need to be in brainstorming mode and capture everything that comes to mind, no matter how outrageous or tangential it may seem. The output from this phase does not go onto your transformation map; rather it sits behind that as context, reminding you of the broad canvass on which you will be painting your strategy.

The wider you scan, the more likely you are to pick up important information that you need to bear in mind as you move towards generating clarity. Here are some key questions to ask yourself:

- Are we under threat, for example, from new technologies, low barriers to entry, social trends, etc.? If so, how? (This a priori question can open out a much wider set of thoughts and responses to the following questions.)

- Why are we doing it this way?

- What other ways can we do this?

- What are we comfortable with?

- Have we become too comfortable? Why?

- What can we change?

- Why not do something completely different?

Don't just think about your competition - think about what new opportunities are out there.

- How can you serve your customers in different ways - ways that your competitors haven't thought about?

- You'll need to get support for your strategy, so think about who in your organization needs to give you the support to get approval. How are you going to persuade them?

- What evidence do you need to persuade these people? Determine that evidence beforehand, gather it, and present it to them when getting their approval.

- Also consider the best timing, not only to approach the people from whom you'll need approval but also in terms of the business planning cycle - can you tag into it? Must you tag into it?

I've given you the basic tools. Be inquisitive. Don't be afraid to ask, "Why? I don't quite get this yet."

Step 2: Focus your strategy.

In the next stage of developing your strategy, you need to start to focus on your options and narrow down what you are going to do. You should be at the point where you understand the marketplace and opportunities, and you've diagnosed the problems in that space. Now you're ready to address the two fundamental questions that every great strategy must answer: "Where do you want to get to?" and "How will you get there?"

For this part of the exercise, try to focus on a sensible, tangible timeframe. I suggest that this should be between one and three years, though in some cases, it makes sense to have a shorter or longer timeframe. Shorter timeframes tend to involve more tactical effort rather than having the overall coherence that great strategy brings, and longer timeframes risk being unachievable due to the large number of unknowable events and circumstances that may intervene. But the choice is yours - choose a timeframe that works best for you and your organization.

Another challenge I sometimes encounter is that people often wait until the business cycle the organization forces on them to think about their future strategy. I personally don't believe great strategy should necessarily be driven by business planning cycles, but I do recognize that it is often only during the annual cycle of reviewing progress, direction, and performance that organizations accept the need to set aside time and to adopt more open-minded ways of thinking about what needs to happen in the future. So don't wait for the business planning cycle to force you into thinking strategically: start now! But if you think the best way of playing your thinking into the organization is to use one of these cycles, then you are best placed to judge that.

To return to the example of the USA putting a man on the moon - people at that time thought it was an unachievable mission. In fact, Kennedy had done a lot of work to make sure that it was achievable and was something that could be done within the allotted space of time (we read this as Kennedy's scanning and focusing).

The strategy essentially focused America's resources on a clear and articulated set of challenges that they knew were achievable within the given timeframe so that they could leapfrog what the Russians were doing. In determining where you want to get to, you too must make sure your end goal is possible. Yes, it should be ambitious but must still be possible. Do take a reality check because I don't want you to sign up to a strategy that's not going to deliver and fail.

Start this exercise by re-clarifying or re-stating your goal. Write it down in just three or four succinct bullet points. Write these bullet points on the top right hand corner of a sheet of A4 paper. And write down a similar set of bullet points to describe your current situation at the bottom left of the page. It should look like so:

Diagram 4: Transformation Map Outline

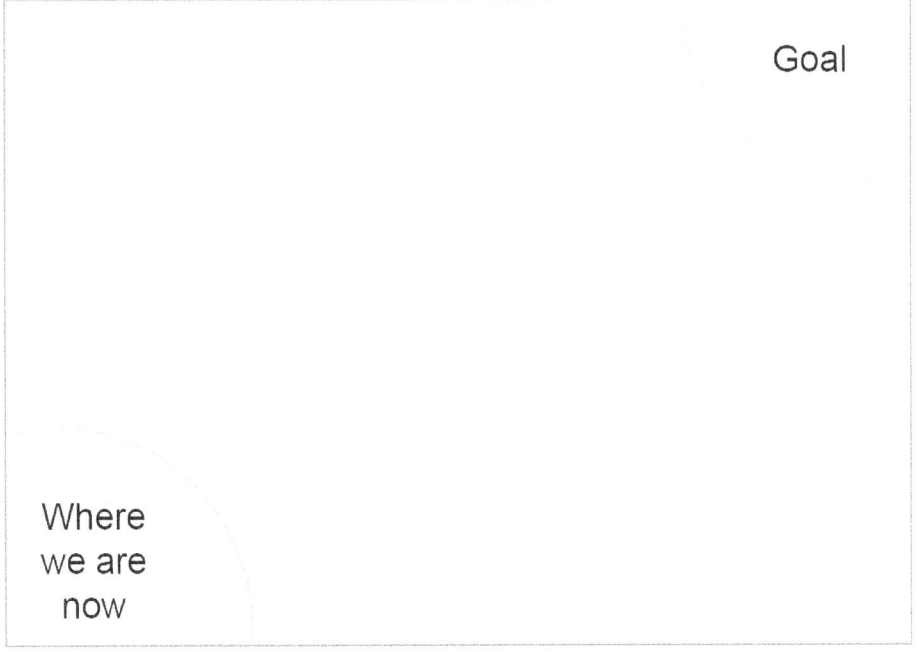

Now that you know where you want to get to, you need to consider how to get there. Your mission, during this exercise, is to work out what the key actions are and to group them into key strategic areas of activity that are going enable you to achieve your goal.

Again, I want you to brainstorm. Write down on sheet of paper, or preferably a set of sticky notes, all of the different actions that you could take in order to help you achieve your goal. Record ideas as if you're talking to someone else. Record hundreds of ideas. Don't worry about practicality - you'll consider that later. Keep going until you feel that you've exhausted the main actions that will need to be covered. You may even want to spread your brainstorming out over a few days to enable you to gather ideas from a wider set of people. The key here is to create a lot of possible actions, bearing in mind that you may not actually do them all. If it helps, consider these questions and articulate responses to them:

- What are the key things that you can do?

- How do you get there?

- What needs to change?

- How are you going to make those changes?

- Who can help you make the changes?

- How are you going to measure progress?

Now look at these actions and try to find three or four groups of work (no more) that you can control or directly influence that will help you move towards your goal. Take some time to work out these groupings, but don't worry about getting them absolutely right just yet. You can change your mind later if you want. What you are looking for here is some sort of guiding structure to frame your strategy - the key themes or sets of actions that will help you achieve the breakthrough you are looking for.

The reason I suggest you limit yourself to three or four main groups of activity is that it forces you to be strategic, to see the guiding themes that will drive your success forward. It forces you to bring focus and clarity to what might otherwise be a jumble of tasks.

Once you are happy with your groupings, place each of your actions into just one of those groups. If something belongs in more than one group, either break it down to smaller chunks of work that can be allocated separately into the relevant category of work, or choose a main home for the action. The important thing in this exercise is to make sure that every task or action has a home so that you can start to see the wood for the trees.

Once you have placed these actions into groups, spread each group of actions out horizontally on a page (you can see why sticky notes make this exercise easier, and you may need to have a piece of brown paper or a sheet of A3 paper to make this exercise easier). The actions on the left of the page are going to be nearer in time and the actions on the right much farther away in terms of time. In this way, you can start to see what needs to happen quickly and which areas of work can wait until later.

The reason for this step in the exercise should be obvious: you're not going to get all the way towards your end goal or ideal state in one quick leap. You will need to build or layer your actions. It is a bit like teaching someone to drive a car: they won't turn into Lewis Hamilton on day one, or even within three months. You are going to need to introduce them to the basics first - using the accelerator, brake, clutch, and gears - before letting them loose on the highway. Only later will you introduce the more complex maneuvers, like hill starts and emergency stops. The person learns more and more with each drive. What you didn't do was chunk it all in one go - you didn't start the person out on a busy, eight-lane freeway in the pouring rain. The person first achieved a level of basic driving and then improved.

Just as driving skills build up over time, your strategy needs to allow you to do the same. You need to carefully stage how you are building up towards your end goal. That's why the element of time is actually very important in thinking through your strategy. You need to thoughtfully determine what it is that you need to achieve by when that's going to enable you to do a certain thing. And check and change.

If it helps in this exercise, and assuming you have a three-year timeframe for your strategy, ask yourself the following questions to decide what needs to happen when:

- Where do you need to be at the end of the next quarter?

- Where do you need to be at the end of the year?

- Where do you need to be at the end of three years?

You will probably notice at this stage in the exercise that there is just too much to do. This is normal. You are going to need to be ruthless if you are going to succeed now. Focus with laser-like clarity on your goal, and strike out actions and tasks that do not add high value in terms of achieving that goal. You should also highlight those that are absolutely essential to achieving your goal, perhaps giving them one, two, or three stars, depending on how key they are. Keep going at this until you have eliminated all of the low-value-add tasks and established a clear and achievable set of actions that will help you move towards your goal.

The final stage in this exercise is to place the mission-critical tasks and any other key activities you feel need to be captured onto a single sheet of paper in the relevant groupings and spread out over time. Again, you may find it easier to do this with brown paper and sticky notes in a workshop-style format for your first pass. If you get it right, this can easily be transposed onto a PowerPoint template.

You can download an editable PowerPoint version of this slide is available on the book website at
http://www.theexecutiveentrepreneur.com/tmap

Diagram 5: Transformation Map Template

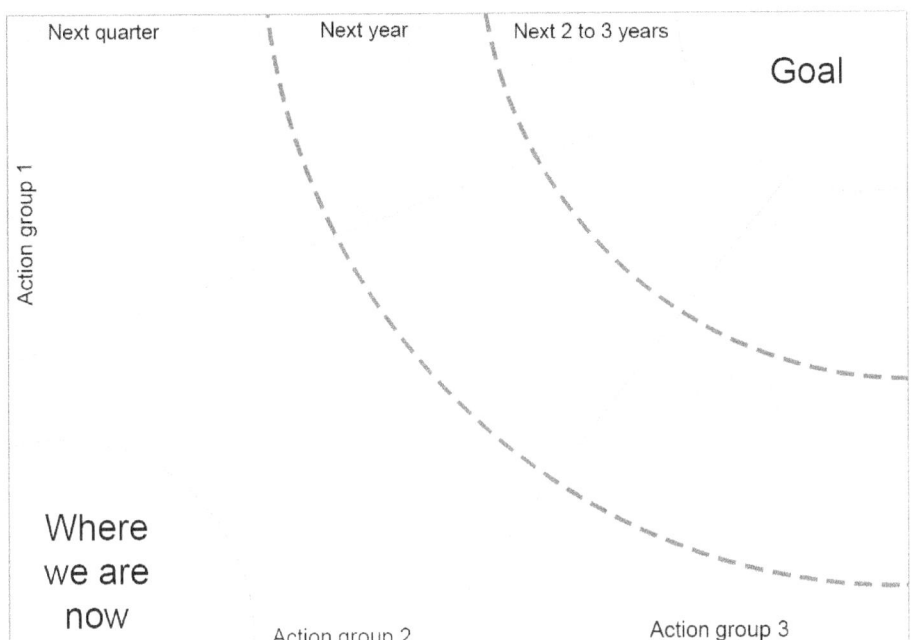

Step 3: Test and refine.

This is the Act phase. You might have expected me to tell you that the first thing you must do is to go and take one of those actions forward. Well, yes, eventually. But I actually want you to start by testing it. Does it make sense to other people? Do they buy into it? What would they change? What do they think?

Don't sit in an ivory tower or even an ivory-towered workshop environment to create your strategy. Go and test it. Test it with a couple of customers. Test it with a couple of people in your supply team. Test it with a couple of trusted advisors that you have outside of your organization. Don't spend a long time doing the testing - you can do it very, very quickly within a week or two.

It's just a few phone calls, a few face-to-face meetings, a few cups of coffee. Test it. Make sure you get different perspectives. That doesn't mean to say you should listen to the last person you speak to - you need to have your own mind and your own presence - but get external perspectives.

Test your strategy and make sure that it's got a sense of solidity that other people will be able to hold onto and get. Keep in mind that it's not going to only involve you alone. You work in an organization, and unless you have the ability to call all the shots in that organization, it's unlikely that the strategy will be something that you alone are responsible and accountable for, so you're going to have to involve and persuade others. Make sure you test it with people who are going to be involved in delivering it and crucially with the decision makers who will need to back it.

So get in gear - start scanning, get focused, and take action.

Shift 3: Create Momentum

Strategy is no good sitting on a shelf. You've got to turn it into action if it is going to mean anything at all. Once you have decided what to do, you have to do it. It really is that simple when you boil it down. So why do so many good intentions get forgotten, why do so many goals get chalked up as pipe dreams rather than brought into reality, and why do so many strategies sit on the shelf?

Here are some of the most common reasons that good intentions fail to be realized:

- We fail to take enough focused action towards our goals because we feel daunted. The key here is to get the ball rolling to conquer our fear.

- We allow ourselves to be distracted by the million other things that are calling for our attention. The key here is to focus.

- We struggle to decide which course of action to follow to achieve our goal and allow ourselves to become stymied by analysis paralysis. The key here is to be decisive.

- We don't make the right adjustments when things don't go according to plan. The key here is to get feedback, reflect, and act on it.

Let's go deeper into each of these.

Get Started

Sometimes big goals can seem daunting to us, and so we simply don't start on the journey, or if we do and come across obstacles, we wander off track, get distracted and lose interest. Now is the time for you to step outside your comfort zone. Taking action requires effort, which people often associate with pain and fear. One of the best ways of moving through this initial pain barrier is to use the exercises we covered in the section on goal setting about harnessing pain and pleasure. I encourage you to refresh your memory on the notes you made there. Look in particular at the notes you made about the good things that will come from your achieving your goals and the pain that you will experience if you don't. This alone might be enough to get you moving. But I want to give you three Executive Entrepreneur challenges to help you get the ball rolling.

Executive Entrepreneur Challenge 9: Harness Your Subconscious

You probably know that your subconscious mind is an incredibly powerful driver of your conscious attention, constantly scanning your environment and alerting you to things that you have programmed it to consider most important to your survival and wellbeing. You need to use this powerful driver to help you take action. This exercise is a very simple but powerful way of doing so.

To harness your subconscious onto achieving your goal, write down your goal and keep it where you can read it morning and evening. Don't just write one sentence - write down what you are going to achieve, why it is important to you, and the key steps that you will take to achieve it. Be clear about your timescale: when will you achieve your goal.

It may take you two or three goes to get this to a point where it begins to resonate strongly with your intuitive sense of it being clear and complete.

Once it has this resonance, write it out in your best handwriting on a clean sheet of A4 paper and keep this somewhere visible so that you can read it first thing in the morning, last thing at night, and at other times of the day too. Writing it out by hand is important; typing it on your computer simply does not have the same resonance. It does not carve it into your subconscious - it delegates it to bits and bytes on your hard drive, and that is not what is going to drive you to take daily action. So write it out.

In this way you embed your goal into your subconscious to train it to start filtering what is going on in your world to help you achieve that goal. It will start to reject distractions and extraneous items, and you will find it easier to keep focused. When you hit challenges, as you most certainly will, it will help you to stay focused and determined on achieving what you want, and you will find it easier to get creative and resourceful in finding ways through the barriers that you face.

I've done this several times, and I have gone to the lengths of buying a nice pen with a thick italic nib and writing on high-quality cartridge paper so that it looks and feels clear, simple, elegant, and important to me. This creates additional resonance and really does help me to keep focused on what it is I want to achieve. I am able to keep that focus more clearly through the days and weeks, as I move towards achieving my goal.

A further build on this exercise is to rewrite your goal every so often as you refine and adjust how you are achieving it. Don't do this too often, however, as it is important to have some constancy in your journey towards your goal. My own experience is that once I have got it right, it is only necessary to revisit and refine it once every three to six months. Sometimes, just rewriting it is all that is necessary with just one or two changes in wording that keep it fresh and tighten it up.

The act of rewriting it carves it back into my subconscious, saying: "This really is important to me and for my wellbeing and that of those I care about. Go to work in remembrance of this."

Executive Entrepreneur Challenge 10: Create a Plan

We looked at creating a roadmap, or transformation map, in the previous section on getting strategic. Now we need to take this down a level, to start to map out how we are going to use our time effectively to achieve our big goals.

For clarity, I am not saying that you have to plan out every single day of the year, but you do have to have some sense of the roadmap if you are going to create momentum and stay on track towards achieving your goals. That means clarifying what you need to do to achieve your goals, putting it into a sensible order, and taking action against that plan.

I'd like you to use the goal-planning template for this exercise. It is available in the Executive Entrepreneur Workbook but you can also use blank pages of your journal if you prefer. For one or more of your key goals, do the following:

- Write down the key milestones or outcomes that need to be ticked off to achieve your goal, and place them into one of the next four quarters of the year, according to when it needs to be achieved by. This will give you a clear sense of the outcomes that you are driving for in each quarter.

- Now, on a second page, do the same for the next three months. This will give you a clear sense of what you need to achieve each month in order to achieve your goals.

- Now, for the first month, map out what needs to happen in each of the four weeks of that month to achieve the outcomes that need to be achieved in that month.

- Now, for the week ahead, write down what needs to happen to achieve your goals for that week. Also spend some time mapping that into your calendar. Carve out chunks of time to allocate to achieving these outcomes and make sure that you protect them in your diary.

A top tip for creating this map is to make sure that you keep a decent amount of white space in your plans. I would advise keeping at least twenty-five percent of your time free from scheduled activities to allow for the bumps and challenges that always arise in everybody's day and life. The mistake some people make is to schedule every second of the day, and when they hit a speed bump, there is absolutely no resilience for them to adjust and cope with what just happened. They go off plan, they get stressed, and you soon know about it if you happen to work with somebody like this because they start dumping that stress onto other people.

So keep some white space in your days so that you can adjust and cope with those speed bumps. It might be hard to achieve in reality, but it is a top tip that I have found increases my productivity because it enables me to stay focused on tasks at hand, knowing that I can tackle the speed bump later in the day when I have allowed myself time for such things.

In this way, you will create a clear map of what you need to do, and you'll have a clear understanding of what you need to do in the week ahead to achieve your goals, as well as a good sense of the work that flows on from that.

Don't expect this to be perfect, by the way. Just get it good enough that you can start to take action with confidence that you are heading in the right direction. We'll talk later in this section about how to give yourself feedback and make adjustments as you go in order to stay on track.

Executive Entrepreneur Challenge 11: Start Small

Another mistake that people make is focusing on the enormity of the task or goal that they set themselves. When they see this big goal, it just seems too big and too hard to achieve, so they don't take action. Alternatively, they feel insufficiently clear about their big goals and their "why," so they do nothing, neither clarifying their mind nor taking action.

The antidote to both of these stymieing challenges is to start small. As the joke we all know reminds us: "How do you eat an elephant? One bite at a time."

In this second very simple kick-starter exercise, I want you to take your goal and write down two or three small things you can do today to move towards it, two or three actions that you can take today which will help bring that goal into reality. Once you have done that, pick one action that is easiest and do it right now. Put this book down and go and do it - whether it takes one minute, one hour, or some other unit of time. The point is to create momentum towards achieving something you care about right now by completing a small action.

Another variation on this is what I call the sixty-second kick starter. It's really a way of tricking your brain into action and momentum. What can you do in the next sixty seconds that will move you towards your goal? Is it powering up your laptop and typing the first few lines of an email to that key contact that can help you? Is it making the phone call to your client that you have been putting off? Just one small thing that you can do now, in this moment, to move you towards your goal creates the momentum and starts to release the energy that will help you take farther, even bigger steps towards your goal. And before too long you'll be running towards your goal.

Flow

You've probably heard a lot about flow and being in a state of peak performance. Some people talk about it like it's a new discovery. But what does it mean? I'm sure you've experienced times of pure concentration, where you're no longer aware of your body or time, you are outside of that, absolutely absorbed and giving your best in that moment: there is only now. When you are in that moment, you are in flow, and almost certainly you are in a state of peak performance.

That state is not new to the human race: it is as old as the human species itself. Sure, there is new science around what it means and how you can measure it. But I think the most interesting fact is that as a species not only have we forgotten how to get ourselves into that state easily and consistently, but also we invent more and more distractions to prevent us from being able to do so.

The good news is that achieving the state of flow is still easily within our grasp and replicable on a consistent basis. And we can use this state to break through to our most important goals to become unstoppable in delivering levels of performance that hitherto we felt were only accessible to those at the top of their games. In short, you too can join those playing at their best. But you need to put the foundations in place first, and that starts with your mindset.

Case Study: The Hunter-Gatherer

The human species exploded from a small primate, capable of adapting and surviving, to one that was capable of thriving. Fossils and bone remains show that the size of our ancestors' skulls and bones grew rapidly in a very short space of time. This was because we were able to consistently find food, in particular, protein, that enabled us to feed, relax, and grow into a wise, loving, and capable species. We did this through consistently achieving a state of flow and peak performance - 40,000 years ago and on up through the ages.

If you haven't seen it already, it's really worth going to look at an extract of a BBC documentary narrated by Sir David Attenborough called "Human Mammal, Human Hunter" (see Bibliography for link), which shows how we used to hunt. This powerful clip follows the San people of the Kalahari Desert. There are only a few of them left, but they still know how to catch prey using the most ancient of methods, persistence hunting. They run their prey down, using incredible intuition, teamwork, and skill honed over hundreds of previous hunts.

The film starts with a group of San hunters choosing their prey - the kudu with the largest and heaviest horns to make sure it will tire. They split it from its herd and run after it. For the first few miles, it remains out of sight, but these hunters track and spot where it runs. They work as a team, fanning out when the trail disappears, rediscovering it, persistently pursuing the animal, which generally remains out of sight. As the older hunters tire, they hand off their water to the younger, fresher-legged hunters to enable the pursuit to continue. And the animal has to keep running, it cannot cool itself as efficiently as the human body can, and eventually it gets exhausted.

These Kalahari bushmen stay in a state of peak flow and performance while chasing the animal down. They can follow seemingly hidden trails - a little broken piece of grass here, a footprint there. They put themselves in a state where they literally feel what that animal would do. There's an amazing sequence in the film where a bushman turns circles in the shade, not chasing the animal down but feeling which way it would run next so that he can pick up the trail again. There is only scanty evidence of where the kudu went, but eventually the two meet, and when they do so, the bushman doesn't need to use any weapon because the animal, exhausted, simply collapses.

There are obvious analogies likening the pursuit hunting case study above to business, but what I want to look at here is the importance of focus and flow. In this scene, there are no distractions: the hunter is not thinking about his Twitter feed or his inbox - those can wait till he gets home.

(I joke here, but I'm guessing it is only time before he has those choices himself; he's already wearing modern sneakers on his feet, as you'll see in the video.)

First, the hunter focuses his conscious mind, and we can do that too. Just as the hunter is constantly scanning his environment, we too should be aware of what is around us but not distracted by it. The hunter, filtering everything coming through his senses, is zoned into following the animal. His conscious mind distinguishes the broken twigs or the soft footprint in the distance. Nothing else is important. Nothing else matters. He is completely focused. And he sees it done. He knows that at the end of the trail, this animal will be there, exhausted, and he only need find it. We too can model this in our work, by eliminating distraction and focusing completely on our end goal, seeing it done, and moving towards it in consistent bursts of focused action.

Second, the hunter harnesses his subconscious mind. Over previous chases he has learned what his body is capable of, and he's conditioned and trained himself to thrive in these circumstances. His subconscious mind knows the effort the chase requires and uses this to pace the hunter, thus helping him push his body hard but not so hard he will fail. Step after step, he senses and determines his energy levels and heat, thus helping him maintain a pace he knows he can sustain to the end. This is true focus and flow, and it is powerful to see. In work too, we need to understand the effort that is required and pace ourselves to make sure we can sustain the effort needed to succeed. We can only burn the candle at both ends for short periods of time; it is far better to pace ourselves and go the distance with a healthy mind and healthy body.

Third, the hunter uses his team. They too desire success, for it will feed them. His win is their win. They hand their water to him as they drop out of the chase, and he knows he has the stamina to finish because he's done it many times before, or perhaps this is his first time he's running as the final hunter. Because he's seen, followed, and watched others do it, he knows how to model that for himself.

And he's constantly acting, checking, and changing course - all in the peak state of flow.

Finally, the hunter repeats what he knows works on a consistent basis. While the film only shows one hunt, the hunter knows that whenever he wants, he can single out another animal and bring home the food, week after week, month after month, drought after drought - because he knows he can consistently outrun the animal. This too is our challenge. We have to do what we know works consistently, day after day and week after week, if we are to succeed in achieving our biggest goals, the ones that drive, motivate, and inspire us. Small steps repeated daily lead to the end goal of our chase, our pursuit, and our lives.

Using these skills, we too can evolve very rapidly in a very short space of time. You too can achieve peak performance and flow. You can see it done, and you're there. That is a fantastic place to be. And my aim is to get you into that state and enable you to harness it consistently, time after time, to achieve your goals.

Success Tips for Flow

- Work in 60 to 90 minute bursts with no distractions.

- Use your first 60 to 90 minute burst of the day to focus on your top priority (not your second or third - and it doesn't matter what else you have planned - make it your top priority).

- During your 90-minute blocks, shut yourself away from the world. Turn off your email and social media feeds. Put your phone on "silent" and place it in a drawer.

- Schedule time for distractions. By this, I mean take a break at the end of 90 minutes and do something different - walk around the office, talk to your friends, give your spouse a telephone call, or check your social media.

But keep things tight - do this for 10 minutes, and then get down to your next 90-minute chunk with no distractions.

- Wear headphones, either with white noise, no noise, or one of those calming tracks that you can download from Amazon for $0.99. I particularly like the sounds of forest rain, for example.

- Set a timer both for the 60 to 90 minute bursts and the 15-minute breaks between bursts.

Executive Entrepreneur Challenge 12: Create Flow Time

The challenge stems directly from the "Success Tips for Flow." Clear the first ninety minutes of your diary for the next week and use this time for your number one priority. If it is impossible to clear 9 am to 10:30 am, then consider alternatives - can you get into work one hour earlier for the next week? Can you do your first hour at home, early in the morning before you go to work?

Celebrate here when you have dedicated the first ninety minutes of each day to achieving your goal. How did it feel to create this focus?

Focus

A key reason people fail to achieve flow, and therefore fail to achieve their goals, is that they get distracted. Can you imagine the bushman hunting down his antelope with his Twitter feed on, his Facebook account open, and his email pinging away with alerts on the top of his screen - together with his phone on "silent" but buzzing away? No way! Instead he announces, "Hey guys, we're out of food: let's go get an antelope!" And if he were really hungry, he would never decide, "No, I've got this other thing to do. I'll go catch it tomorrow!"

Distraction and procrastination don't work for the bushman and don't work for you either. But you already know that. So the first thing you need to recognize is that you're in a war, right now, with lots of different distractions. Everyone is competing for your attention and your time, so your challenge is to stay one hundred percent focused on your top goals, no matter what else tries to intervene.

The average person now checks his or her smart phone dozens of times per day. Why? Because we get gratification and instant satisfaction from knowing that someone else out there wants to talk to us. But it is their agenda they want to talk about, not ours. And it does not help us produce what we need in the day.

It can take between ten and fifteen minutes to get fully back into task following an interruption, and we rarely get more than one extended period of uninterrupted time in the day. Think about your own days if you doubt this. The cost of these interruptions is significant. It can take up to twice as long to complete a task when interrupted, and it will often contain more mistakes or be less powerful as a result.

Watch yourself after an interruption, and you'll notice it's true. Sure, you'll go back to doing whatever you were doing, but it won't be with the same intensity and focus for at least a few minutes. So if you're distracted ten times in an hour by incoming emails, texts, and phone calls, as many of us are, then the chances of your achieving any peak productivity during that hour is zero.

You have to eliminate these distractions. Period.

Distractions are an addiction, an opiate, and they completely destroy your concentration and flow. Like any drug, you need to kick the habit if you've not done so already. The exercises below will help you do this.

Success Tips for Focusing

To help you to stay on your own agenda:

- Create a **Golden Hour** before the start of each working day just for yourself. Many advocate a 5 am start to make sure there are no other distractions, but whatever time you pick, make sure that you have at least sixty minutes of pristine, clear quiet time to do your inner work. It can even be helpful to structure this golden time.

- **Morning Motion**: before you do anything else, start your day with some exercise to flush endorphins into your system and get rid of the stress hormones that many of us live with as a background state of being. The only time I skip it is when I know I'm going to be exercising later in the day - and on those days I still struggle to get peak productivity before I have exercised, so I really try not to skip my morning routine.

- **Reflect and Plan for the Day Ahead**: journaling is absolutely key. You must write down your thoughts, worries, concerns, affirmations, gratitude, decisions, goals, and so on. Get it down in ink. It's such a powerful tool for you to look back on and see the progress you've made. Research shows that as you write out your goals and affirmations, they become further embedded into your psyche - remember that and make sure you're getting the good stuff down. As Tony Robbins reminds us, "What's wrong is always available - and so is what's right."

- **Learn a Little**: learning tends to get squeezed out of everyone's daily routine, but it is essential for growth. Sometimes we learn by doing - and that is where the journal can help us reflect and grow. But sometimes we learn by understanding other people's insights and wisdom, whether that's by reading a book, watching a TED Talk, or listening to an audiobook. Always be learning. Always be inquisitive. Who knows where your new insight or next big idea will come from?

- **Distraction-Free Zone**: in your ninety-minute blocks of peak productivity time, don't allow any distractions. If you work in an open-plan office, put on your earphones and listen to some white noise. As I already noted, I find it helpful to put on the sound of tropical rain. People will think twice before bothering you when you have those headphones on; plus, the rain is soothing, helping to create calmer brainwave patterns that enable you to focus even more and produce your best work.

- **Eat that Frog:** make sure you put the first ninety minutes of the working day aside to focus on your number one priority - perhaps the one that you've even been avoiding because it's a big challenge. As my coach says: "Eat that frog!" And that top priority is likely not necessarily the most urgent thing you have to deal with. Remember that a priority is about both urgency and importance - and if you don't focus on the really important but less urgent things, then chances are that these won't get done or won't be done as well as they could be. So spend time on one of your G-level Graduation goals for the year in your first ninety minutes.

With these thoughts in mind and because establishing focus is at the heart of your productivity, here is a set of Executive Entrepreneur Challenges to improve your focus:

Executive Entrepreneur Challenge 13: Chunk Your Time

While I've already talked about the importance of the 60- to 90-minute blocking of your time, I want to approach the concept from a slightly different angle here. A key to staying focused is to create blocks of time where you know you will be able to eliminate distraction and be in flow. The human brain is capable of concentrating for between 60 and 90 minutes at best. So you need three, or ideally four, 90-minute blocks of pure concentration each day, separated by at least 10 minutes where you can take calls or check emails. In those 90-minute blocks, make sure you've already set the agenda for what you want to accomplish so that you can control and monitor your concentration. Use the natural concentration cycle to your advantage.

Again let me repeat this recommendation: spend 90 minutes early in the day working on your top goal with no distractions. That means turning off your Twitter feed, turning off your email, turning off your phone, giving it to your PA or locking it in your drawer - and just focusing for 90 minutes on your core goal. Do that early in the day, once you've set up the day and cleared off any immediate problems that you need to handle - but make sure you do it. I like to block out 9:00 to 10:30 in my diary. I know that that time is the core time that I've got for my number one priority.

It's amazing what you can achieve if you just spend five 90-minute blocks in a week - you've got a whole day plus - on your number one goal. That is an awesome amount of time, and by starting your day in this manner, it creates momentum for the rest of the day. If you work in this way throughout the day, in 60- to 90-minute chunks of time where you stay in a peak state of flow with no distractions and take breaks to refresh your energy and concentration in between, you will achieve amazing things.

Executive Entrepreneur Challenge 14: Eliminate Distractions

Not only do you need to set your own agenda, but you also need to stay on it - no matter what hits you. You have to major on the majors. If you keep your email and your phone on, you're asking to get distracted.

When dealing with potential distractions, a great habit that will help you stay focused is to ask yourself these two questions: How will this serve me? How will this move me towards my goal?

By asking yourself these questions every time you consider a potential distraction, two things happen. First, you remind yourself what you goal is and reconnect with the good feelings that you associate with achieving it. This helps you stay focused. Second, you look for the value in the task. If this value is absent or weak, for example, because it is someone else's agenda rather than yours, then you have a red light flashing, immediately warning you, "This is not helpful to me!" This will help you prioritize more effectively and say no more often, albeit politely.

Executive Entrepreneur Challenge 15: Stick to Your Own Agenda

There's this great story about a consultant way back in the 1920s who was giving some advice to a businessman. When the businessman urged him, "Tell me how much you want me to pay you," the consultant replied, "Don't pay me now. You can pay me later, but give me what you think this advice is worth." A few weeks later, the consultant got a check for 25 thousand dollars, a huge amount of money back in those days. And the consultant had only given the businessman this one piece of advice: Set your day's agenda the evening before, and then stick to that agenda.

What a fantastic story about being clear about your own agenda. It forced the businessman to think with deeper thought and insight about what his priorities were. And that is what I want you to do too.

My advice to you: each evening, in your journal write down the three to five things that you want to do the following day. Three to five things - no more. (The evening is reckoned to be the best time of the day because, apart from allowing you to focus on your priorities without the distraction of work, it should also allow your mind to preprocess the following day's work as you sleep.) And the following day, do those things. Keep to your own agenda.

Executive Entrepreneur Challenge 16: Develop the Habit of Focused Action

The chances are you are already doing some of the above things, at least in part or sometimes. The key to success, in creating focus and momentum, is to ingrain those behaviors so that they become habits that you don't even have to think about. They become just the way that you do things.

There are a lot of different views kicking around the web about how long it takes to establish a habit. Some people say two or three weeks, but it's actually a lot longer than that. The University College of London found it took sixty-six days to install a new habit. That means for the next sixty-six days, for the next two months, you've got to focus on taking daily massive action towards your top goals. So for the next two months, here is my challenge to you to create daily focused action:

- Block out at least one 90-minute block each working day for the next 66 days and guard that block with your life. Use it to take focused action, with absolutely no distractions, towards a single goal that is important to you. Lock away your phone, switch off your email, put your headphones on, or shut the door to signal to your colleagues that you are busy.

- Journal about this each evening. You'll find it useful to give yourself feedback, encouragement that you are making progress, and information about what more you need to do to make even better use of that time tomorrow.

Be Decisive

Often if you spend time analyzing things, you will find that it is not entirely clear which of two or three options is the best one to take. Assuming you've done enough homework and that further analysis is not going to help you, you will recognize that you have reached a point we call "analysis paralysis." You feel stymied and uncertain which option to choose. If you move in one direction, it may be wrong. The key here is to make a decision, to learn from that decision, and to be prepared to adjust if it proves that a different course is better. This is illustrated brilliantly in what I call "The General's Dilemma."

Case Study: The General's Dilemma

There's a great story about General Norman Schwarzkopf, which I picked up from Tony Robbins. This story happened when General Schwarzkopf was a junior member of staff working for another three-star general. It goes back a little way when the three-star general was looking at the future of the military. He had two teams analyzing what should be done. Those two teams had spent over a year each looking at the different problems, and they'd come up with two different strategies to govern the future of the United States military investment.

It wasn't clear which strategy was right, so the teams presented to the general. The first team argued, "Well, these are the scenarios and issues that we've looked at, and we think it looks like this, so this is what we should do . . ." Then the second team presented. Within half an hour the general announced, "Gentlemen, thank you very much for your time. I've listened carefully. We're going for the first option. We're going for scenario number one and strategy number one."

The teams looked at him and asked, "Are you sure? Are you're sure that you want to do that one because it's quite a finely balanced argument? We're not sure that either one of us is right, that either set is right." The general responded, "No, I've made my decision. I'm very clear. We're going for strategy number one. Meeting adjourned."

Afterwards when General Schwarzkopf had the opportunity, he approached the general and inquired, "Sir, how could you make such a quick decision based on such a finely balanced argument?" The general explained, saying, "Son, we got to the point where we had two clear options, but we couldn't learn anything more about which one's right, so I had to make a decision. I had to be decisive. From that decision, we will start to learn which option is right. And if I made the wrong decision, then we can adjust."

Of course the case study is not a verbatim quote of the conversation, but the story is true, and I hope is of some service to you when you face problems in your strategy and you're not clear which way to go. Provided the options on the table are viable, if you're not certain which way to go, then try being decisive. Start moving in one direction. If you're wrong, then you can always adjust.

Adjust

Think about a mechanic fixing a car engine. He has a good understanding of how the engine should work, and he knows enough about the diagnostic tests that he needs to run in order to find out what is not currently working and how to fix it. He runs those tests and starts to fix the engine. As it starts to work again, he gets down to fine-tuning it so that it runs efficiently and smoothly for the owner.

So it is with you and achieving your goals: you should by now have a clear idea of where you want to get to and how to get there. If you've not completed the momentum exercise on creating a map of what you need to do, please do that now.

Now you need to start to give yourself feedback on how you are doing. The following exercises tie in with some of the previous ones, and you can run them together. I've put them down in this order to create clarity for you, but you will find your own rhythm and way of making them work for you.

To adjust you need to have three things:

- A clear understanding of where you want to get to

- An idea of how to get there

- Feedback on how you are doing

Executive Entrepreneur Challenge 17: Daily Review

At the end of each day, review what happened honestly. Celebrate the successes that you have achieved. Be grateful, even for small things.

In this way you create the mindset you need to focus on success, which is your goal.

Now look at whether there are things that you wanted to do or achieve that need to be carried forward. What do you need to do differently tomorrow to make it just that little bit more impactful than today? Remember that better never ends, and small daily improvements stack up to massive momentum over time. So work out what is going to make tomorrow just that bit better.

Become Unstoppable

If you follow these steps and focus on your Graduation goals, particularly and always within the first ninety minutes of each working day without any distractions, I guarantee that you'll amaze yourself. Within a week, you'll be feeling like a different person, and within thirty days, you'll wonder how you ever worked in a different way to this.

Remember to carve out days where you have four periods of ninety minutes in a day, so six hours of peak time. That's pretty much all anyone can ask for. During that time, discard all distractions: no email, no Twitter feed, and no Facebook. For anything that tries to intrude, ask, "How does this serve me?" Review your day and set up the following day. Review your week and set up the following week. Every quarter, review progress against your goals; and at least once a year, if not twice, review your overall goals.

This is establishes focus and drive. This establishes clarity. This establishes peace of mind and the ability to get things done. This is peak performance mindset and behavior, and you will be unstoppable when you are in this space.

Executive Entrepreneur Challenge 18: Turn Strategy into Action

If you have not already done so, download the workbook and resources that go with it and work through the exercises in this section on strategy for one or more of your key strategic challenges at work. You can apply it to other areas of your life too, but that's a whole other book.

It really is worth spending time and effort on this, and it is one of the key exercises and tools that I use in working with organizations.
If you can complete this exercise well, you will create insight, focus, and direction for your team and your organization.

You will be able to walk into the boardroom or the all-staff meeting and say, "This is where we are going, this is what we need to achieve, and here is how we are going to do it." You will multiply one hundred-fold the chances of success. And, crucially, you will have established the foundation for next key shift, which is all about creating momentum.

Take Your Journey Farther!

Download your FREE workbook, join one of my coaching groups, meet like minded individuals, and work through challenges together!

Find out more at:
www.theexecutiveentrepreneur.com

Chapter 4 - Peer Set

Much is written in the personal development literature about the importance of making sure that you put the right people around you to ensure your success. In my experience, there is a huge amount of truth in this. However, in organizations it is not always possible to pick every member of your peer set personally. We must, therefore, find ways to get the most out of what we are given and to recognize when and how to make changes both in our own personal styles and in whom we put around us. That is the focus of this chapter.

There are two key shifts covered within this chapter. Shift 4 looks at how to get the most out of your peer set within your immediate work context, and Shift 5 looks at how to extend your peer set so that you raise the bar on your own performance. Both these shifts are often overlooked and misunderstood. While I have put this chapter in the latter part of the book, it is the one that has the potential to really unleashing your own success as an Executive Entrepreneur way beyond the limits of your own capabilities.

Shift 4: Unleash Your Team

All leaders want to get the most out of their teams. If leaders don't, then they should really rethink or step down. But how many leaders actually manage to tap the full potentials of their teams? It is a tough challenge, and I've seen many people struggle and get frustrated. Common challenges include:

- **Working in silos:** even in small organizations, people and teams can become blinkered and have a tendency to work in silos. It can be more comfortable to keep your head down and get on with what you think is your day job or priority rather than take a wider perspective and act in the organization's best interests. Harder still, people may think they are acting in the organization's best interests when really they are pursuing personal agendas such as marking themselves out for promotions or simply protecting turf.

- **Egotistical behavior:** alpha male behavior is common within executive teams in boardrooms. While focus and drive are key to getting things done, egos and pride can often get in the way of clear thinking and good judgment.

- *Lack of clarity about goals and priorities:* when organizations have multiple goals and priorities, it can often be confusing and difficult for teams and individuals to be clear about what is most important and how to balance competing priorities. For example, I have seen organizations struggle to serve customers effectively because of confusion and internal competition for scarce resources, such as investment capital or IT development resources.

- *Poor communication:* this is at the heart of most critical failures in delivering great service or effective change. Look at any report investigating a failure in public service or lessons learned from a difficult or challenging change program, and you will see poor communication showing through in some shape or form. From the top down, it is incumbent on every leader in the organization to communicate clearly and to ensure that what he or she says is understood and acted on. Easier said than done, I know, but there is a way as I outline below.

And the list goes on! I could keep writing at length about the challenges that leaders face in pulling together people from disparate backgrounds with varying experiences of life and business in different motivations and drivers. But you get the point. The real question is - how do you recognize and tackle these challenges? How do you bring order to confusion when chaos and competition are often the default or mean reversion positions?

The following model on unleashing your team was devised by a great friend of mine, an organizational psychologist named Eric Fleming from Australia. It is particularly useful when you're trying to create change across an organization. Together, we have introduced the thinking to a wide range of leaders from across the globe and have found it resonates strongly with leaders of all cultures and companies. Eric is writing a book on this subject, but for now he has endorsed this treatment of it.

There are five levels that you need to pass through in sequence if you are to unleash your team. You have to make sure that each stage is in place before you move to the next. Too many leaders move straight to being challenging and critical, without working through the earlier stages of the process, and wonder why they don't get the results and performance that they want. They mistakenly think that they can tap into people's inner drive and motivation, and get the best out of them by shouting louder or being more harsh when really all they are doing is demotivating and tearing apart the cohesion that they so badly need. So let's step through each level in turn and make sure we fully understand what is involved in building that level of cohesion successfully.

The stages are:

Level 1: Establish - with roles, responsibilities, and priorities

Level 2: Engage - with vision and understanding

Level 3: Enable - with knowledge, skills, and resources

Level 4: Empower - with responsibility and accountability

Level 5: Unleash - with challenge and support

Case Study: Steve Jobs

Steve Jobs was an outstanding leader. He had many quirks and difficult aspects to his character, but he shifted everybody's perception about what could be achieved within a lifetime and within a company, and for me, that is great leadership. And he applied the model that we've been talking about here.

People think about him as an incredibly challenging leader who came in right from the beginning and started throwing his weight around and challenging, but he wasn't such a caricature in reality. In reality, he applied each stage of the model brilliantly and ruthlessly to give his company massive competitive advantage in the marketplace.

When he set up Apple, he understood that he needed to have different people on his team. Steve Wosniak, the brilliant computer designer, and Ronald Wayne, the gifted "adult supervisor," were lynchpins, but he also needed others to help him with other elements of the design and production.

He established clear roles and responsibilities, right from the get-go. He brought the best people in and made sure that they understood what it was that they were supposed to do (Level 1: Establish - with roles, responsibilities, and priorities).

He created a compelling vision (Level 2: Engage - with vision and understanding), which everyone in his company understood and bought into. Sure, this adapted and evolved as the company grew and technology changed, but it always centered on creating insanely great products in terms of design, operation, and ease of use. They didn't need to be first in the market necessarily. He wasn't the first into the PC market or the digital music market, but he knew that his company's edge was making these products work way better than the competition, and then the company leveraged that position to great effect.

So, Apple was not the first to sell MP3 players, but Steve Jobs was the first to really understand and be able to leverage the revolution these players offered to the music industry. It was iTunes, rather than the iPod, which really propelled the company into the stratosphere, and the whole product suite created a positive spiral, hooking people in with one device and then selling them on to another. It was his vision, which he kept fresh and compelling, that provided a core foundation for the company's success.

But he also needed to deliver results fast. And so he enabled his team with the right knowledge, skills, and resources (Level 3: Enable - with knowledge, skills, and resources). For example, when he built the Apple Mac, he brought together the best team from the company and put them on this, literally pulling them off other less important projects and giving them the responsibility and accountability for delivering (Level 4: Empower - with responsibility and accountability).

Once these foundations were in place, he was then able to use his incredibly challenging nature and powerful insights to drive his teams incredibly hard (Level 5: Unleash - with challenge and support) to deliver new products and establish change and growth incredibly rapidly, not only in his own organization but across a whole range of industries that Apple helped to transform. He was very challenging and supportive of his team as they drove for excellence. He would challenge when he wasn't happy; he would listen to his instincts, but he would also support his team and find ways through unblocking those challenges.

For example, he used to bring his top team together once a week every week to look at how the different areas of work and technology development in each division could be applied to the products that they were developing. By bringing his team together in this way, they were able to support and enable each other to succeed as he challenged them to deliver to even greater heights.

This model can also be used to better understand some of the difficulties Jobs had in his first stint at Apple, leading up to his being ousted from the company. There was a mix of trouble amongst his senior team with difficulties at the Level 2 (some board members did not share Jobs' vision for insanely great products, good was acceptable, and a proliferation of average products ensued), Level 3 (arguably the CEO appointment of John Scully III, whose background was in marketing Pepsi, was not the best hire for an innovative technology company on a massive growth curve), and Level 4 (the CEO and others began to feel undermined and threatened by Jobs' persistent pursuit of his own agenda). These cracks, at each level of the model, led to senior board members being able to oust Jobs from his post. Leaders beware! Reflect on each level of this model and ask yourself - how can I fix trouble at each level? Remember - they are all key.

Steve went on undiminished to set up Next, revive Pixar, and make a triumphant return to Apple in due course, rescuing it from bankruptcy with only two or three months of cash flow to spare. So, even the darkest of boardroom coups can have a silver lining.

Level 1: Establish - With Roles, Responsibilities, and Priorities

You've heard the phrase "get the right people on the bus." Pause for a moment and think about what this means. As Jim Collins pointed out in his work studying hundreds of companies that went from good to great performance, all great performance comes from getting the right people into your organization and working with them to establish where you are going to go and how to get there.

Many leaders make the mistake in thinking that they have to start with their own visions. They get their megaphones out and tell people, "This is where we are going! Come on, get on board, let's get moving!" But great change does not start this way. Sure, the leader must have ambition and drive for the organization and a desire to achieve greatness.

But she does not need to have all the answers. She does need to know how to assemble a great team who can help create the map and clarify how the organization needs to shift in order to grow. This is a skill, a foundational skill, and one that every leader must take seriously.

To simplify things, leaders may need to build their teams from one of two positions. Either the bus is empty and they have the privilege of being able to hire new people to join them, or the bus is already partially or completely full.

In the first case, change may happen more quickly provided the leader is able to hire well. In the latter, it may take more time or require some tough decisions. But in both cases there are some common approaches, tools, and techniques that can be used effectively to help you make your decisions. Here are four that I found to be most effective:

- **Know your own strengths and weaknesses**: we like to hire people like us, but this is often not the best approach to building your team. Such practice means that we end up with a leadership team that possesses the same strengths and the same weaknesses. A room full of alpha males is a complete nightmare for any chief executive to work with, as many I have worked with know. Far better to start by understanding your own strengths and weaknesses, and hire to complement those. For example, if you know that you are weak in completing and finishing tasks in project managing through the detail, then find someone in your leadership team who is great at that and leverage that skill.

- **Know what your ideal team looks like**: it is fairly standard practice these days to conduct a skills audit of your team and to build training development to fill gaps. While this may feel like forward progress, it is actually a fairly sterile and laborious way into the problem of creating a great leadership team. A much more insightful way is to take a step back and ask yourself what you really want in your leadership team. What strengths, skills, and abilities do you need to have in place in order to succeed? Map this out and compare what you have against your ideal team, not through a skills audit but through simple assessment of strengths and weaknesses - something that you can do using your own pen and paper in a quiet morning. This will give you great clarity as you decide how to build the team that you need.

- **Hire and promote the best**: this may go without saying, but if you want average performance, then hire average people. If you want great performance, look for great people. This may mean that you need to offer above average wages and incentives. The massive benefit this gives you is that it gives you the right to expect great performance, something that sets your own mindset as well as those you hire when it comes to delivering change and improvements.

- **Focus on whom your reports hire:** I learned this from a highly successful CEO who had generated twenty years of successive growth in dividend payments for his shareholders. In addition to identifying opportunities for growth for his company, he explained that the secret of his success was based on paying close attention to the people that his direct reports hired. He had no doubt that he had hired the best direct reports. After all he knew what he wanted, and he'd gone out and found it in the people he had hired. However each of those people in turn had direct reports - perhaps a hundred in all. It was those hires that the CEO also focused on. He wanted to know that the these people were also of the highest caliber, so he ensured that he was directly involved in their recruitment and in how they were supported once in the organization. This paid dividends, metaphorically and physically, in terms of his organization's growth and success.

You and your team will need to recognize and handle change: as your organization grows and develops, new challenges and opportunities will arise, and you will have to continue to clarify roles, responsibilities, and priorities. This is not a once-a-year activity. It needs to happen as and when the need arises, which is often not in line with annual appraisals. Make sure that your staff recognizes and embraces this, and you'll find handling change a much more collaborative and open process.

This is a fairly directive stage of team building, one in which you are going to be fairly prescriptive about your requirements, challenging and searching until you are comfortable that they are met, at least in the main. You may never be entirely satisfied that you are there, which is probably a good thing because it means that you are thinking about the next level of performance and growth. Embrace this discomfort, work with it, and keep a close eye on the composition of and interplay within your team: this is the absolute foundation of your performance and that of your organization.

Executive Entrepreneur Challenge 19: Review Your Team

Here is a simple exercise that takes you through key points from this foundational level of unleashing your team. Set aside at least half an hour to complete it, regardless of how nascent or mature your team is.

Step 1: Assess your own strengths and weaknesses.

With a blank sheet of paper in front of you or your journal, spend a few moments to gather your thoughts and then write down from your gut what you think your strengths and weaknesses are as a leader and manager of your team. Put strengths on the right hand side of the page and weaknesses on the left. When thinking about this, it helps to avoid focusing on the solutions. Just take a step back and reflect and let the process work. If it helps, ask yourself the following questions:

- When I have achieved my greatest results, what was I doing that was awesome? What did I get right? What did other people notice about my strength and skills?

- When I have my clearest thoughts and vision in mind, what is it that I'm doing that is different from the day-to-day maelstrom of activity?

- When I feel frustrated, weak, or powerless what is going on? What character traits am I exhibiting?

- What do I think my fatal flaws are? What really inhibits me or hampers me from achieving more of my full potential?

Step 2: Describe your ideal top team.

Now I want you to taken another blank page in your journal and use it to describe the ideal team reporting to you. Write down short, simple answers to the following questions:

- How big is the team?

- How do they balance my strengths and weaknesses?

- How do they work together? And how do they work with those who report to them? How do they collaborate to get things done?

- What is the balance of characters it contains? Does it have a mix of extroverts and introverts, visionaries and completer-finishers, leaders who are good with people, networkers, mavericks, and people who can nail the detail and get things done?

- What specific roles do you need in your top team? And what specific skills and strengths do you need in each role? Write this down, role by role.

- What are the qualities and strengths of the reports that they need to hire or have in place? Write down short notes against each of the key roles in your ideal top team.

Step 3: Assess your team against this profile.

Against this page of notes, use a simple system of ticks and crosses to assess how well your current team fits against your ideal profile. Consider not only your top team but also their reports. Keep a wide perspective for this exercise.

Use one, two, or three ticks to indicate the strength of fit with your idea requirements; and one, two, or three crosses to indicate the strength or size of the gap or challenge. This will give you a simple visual clue to where your focus needs to go in getting the right people on board.

Step 4: Action plan

Reflect again on what this exercise is telling you. Create a simple action plan by answering the following questions:

- What do you need to change?

- Whom do you need to hire?

- Whose minds or attitudes do you need to challenge or stretch?

- Which people do you need to have tough conversations with? Are there any you think you may need to let go? What do you need to do to prepare for these conversations?

- How are you going to get a grip on whom your reports hire?

A final thought on this exercise comes from a quote I picked up along the way:

> *It's not the people you hire that will sink your business;*
> *it's the people you don't fire.*

This is the one of the hardest parts of being a leader. You have to be prepared, if necessary, to exercise tough love. You have to make sure that you have people with you who are either extremely capable or can quickly grow into the roles that you need to fill. Where people are a long way short of the mark, it is likely that they will be depressed, unhappy, and stressed individuals. It may be that some of these people will flourish in a different environment. You don't need me to lecture you on this, but you do need to steel yourself. Getting it right at this foundational stage will allow you to be challenging and supporting at the higher levels of unleashing your team. You will get a lot more pleasure and satisfaction in the long run by getting your foundations rock-solid. It starts here and it starts now!

Level 2: Engage - With Vision and Understanding

You have to create a compelling vision and ensure that your team understands it. People talk about a burning platform often. What is the absolute priority that is going to galvanize and focus a team on success? Can you paint that clear vision of the future? Spend some time setting that down if you haven't done so already. Where possible get your team to help define and flesh out the vision or bits of it. Think about what it is that you need to achieve in your workplace. Determine the big shift that your team is going to make over the next three months, six months, or even a year, and convey that vision to them so that they really can feel and touch and sense what difference needs to happen over the coming period.

With that in mind, they will begin to engage themselves, and as I wrote earlier in this book about engaging your heart, so you need to engage your team's heart. You need to find what it is that taps into their passion and drive. They should be in this job for a reason, and you need to connect with that and convey what it is that you're creating together that is way stronger than what they could achieve separately. This is something that Gina Bradbury, the person in this book's opening case study, did incredibly effectively. In transforming her organization's performance in supporting young people, she connected completely with the why of the workers, team, and organization. Everyone that turned up to work was committed to making a difference for young people. How could they help young people create a better set of decisions around their future so that more people were able to make the right choices and succeed more effectively for themselves?

This was an absolutely clear and compelling vision - that they could do a much better job of this by providing a much fuller and richer set of information for young people but also, crucially, by providing really great advice and support to the young people to enable them to think through their options carefully and understand better the consequences of different decisions so that they could make a decision that suited them well.

Gina created this compelling vision for her team. She showed them how what they were doing at the time was good but not good enough and that there was a much better outcome that they could create for young people. Once the people in her organization connected with her compelling vision and understood it, they understood how their roles would contribute to it and how they could start to prioritize their time. So again, building on those roles and responsibilities, and connecting with that vision, Gina made sure that she had a very strong platform to move on through.

Once your team has connected, engaged, and committed to your vision, then you are ready to move on to the next level of unleashing your teams.

Executive Entrepreneur Challenge 20: Creating an Engaging Vision and Plan

Here is an exercise that you can do which will help you engage and involve your team in creating a vision and strategic plan if you don't have one already, or which you can adapt to help refine and refresh the one that you do have.

Step 1: Gather your thoughts.

Prior to engaging your team, I want you to gather your thoughts. Write down your own vision of what you want your team to achieve in the year. Hone this and rewrite it until you are broadly happy with it. Don't wordsmith it because it is really just for your benefit right now.
In the second step is when you will start to engage your team in refining it.

Against this vision, brainstorm out what your strategic priorities are for achieving it. Try and boil this down to no more than three priorities; more than three and it gets confusing for people to hold onto and it is moving away from being strategic.

Against each of your strategic priorities, write down the top-line things that need to happen to achieve them. If it helps, use the goal-setting exercise of thinking backwards: looking back at the end of the year, what needs to happen to have made that year awesome in terms of achieving your strategic priorities?

Step 2: Engage your team.

Set aside at least half a day in which you and your top team will work together to clarify your strategic priorities and what needs to happen against them. Ideally I would recommend doing this off-site so that they are freed up from the pressures and stresses of work.

Running such workshops is an art in itself, so do consider getting external facilitation for this. As the leader, you also want to be able to play a full role in the discussion and co-creation of the vision and strategy. While the facilitator's pen is a very powerful tool, you may want someone else skilled to wield it, thus enabling you to be more present with your team.

Level 3: Enable - With Knowledge, Skills, and Resources

Once you have a clear vision and a clear understanding of what you need to achieve, the next step is to make sure that you have enabled your team to deliver it. And to enable your team to succeed, you have to make sure that they have the resources, skills, and knowledge needed to succeed. This is a very basic, simple statement but fundamental to achieving your success.

Knowledge and skills can be acquired, either through development or hiring. So look at your team, think carefully about whom you have, what they know, and the skills that they have, and think about how you're going to give them the boost in those areas that they need to succeed in terms of achieving your vision. And this is not just about training. It needs to be about how to apply learning, knowledge and skills to get the outcome you need. Knowledge alone is useless. It must be applied; otherwise it is just information that sits somewhere in your library or brain, "shelf help" as I've heard it called.

So think carefully about your team, and think creatively around them and how you can not only develop their skills and knowledge but get them to apply it as well. In particular, think about investing in high-quality coaching - both for you and them. This is part of the fifth shift that I talk about below, and it is a game-changer. If you don't have coaching in place for yourself or your top team, you are missing out on a massive opportunity for a step change in performance for minimal investment in comparison to the results you will achieve (provided you hire the right coach and take appropriate action!).

One thing I find that can help is to sit down and literally list out individuals within your team and look at your vision and the roles that you've carved out for them. This can take a bit of time, but it's absolutely essential if you're going to unleash your team to succeed. Think and talk to them about:

- Their knowledge and skills and the application of them: both now and what more they need to know and what more they need to do in order to succeed. How can you help them achieve these?

- The resources they can leverage: these may include time, funding, access to other people within the organization, and externals, such as a coach or mentor. You need to think about how you can, as a leader, carve out those resources for that team and that individual. If it's time from other parts of the organization that they need, make sure you secure it. If they need confirmation of funding, make sure you get it.

Again, this is something that Gina did exceptionally well. Looking around at her team, she understood that with the major shifts that had to be made in terms of gathering information from the outside world into the system, there was a big resource gap that was simply about time and effort.

There wasn't enough time and resources within the team to meet that, so Gina placed top priority on securing this resource, which required approval from the board and executive team. She was allocated funding to hire temporary staff and approval to work with a much wider range of third party organizations willing to bring their own resources and insight to the service.

Gina took a very powerful, creative, and innovative approach to making sure that her project was appropriately resourced. Literally within a couple of months, her team managed to triple the data held by the organization about courses that young people could apply for. They moved from a very partial coverage of the country to a complete coverage of the country, in terms of what courses were captured and held in their system.

So, just like Gina, you must think creatively about how you plug your resource gaps. Don't just think about cash. Think about whom you can partner with. Think about whom you can draw into your organization on a partnership basis - who else might be willing to contribute in return for being associated with you and your service, product, or other market offering? There are lots of different ways that you can join resources.

Another really good, simple way of finding resources when there is not enough to go round is simply to de-prioritize another activity. If you say something else can simply wait or you can accept a lower quality of delivery in other areas, you can create time and space for your absolute number one priority.

Case Study: Our Kalahari Bushmen

Let's also look at how the Kalahari bushmen applied the model for unleashing their teams. If you watch the video about pursuit hunting (see Bibliography for link) and see how the bushmen are operating, they've got peer roles and responsibilities in place (Level 1: Establish - with roles, responsibilities and priorities). For example, they know the younger man (but not the youngest) with the strong legs and the experience will finish the hunt. But the others also have their roles too. They help to track, making sure that the initial chase is efficient and strong and that they bring their wisdom of many, many, many pursuit hunts before to bear. They also carry water and hand it on to the front-runner when they tire, so he can carry on the chase. They all share a vision of the goal - food for their families - which engages their hearts and drives them on to success (Level 2: Engage - with vision and understanding). They are acutely aware of their responsibility to feed their families. If they don't bring home meat, they know people are going to be hungry, and this spurs them on to amazing levels of focus and achievement.

They have built up the knowledge about how to track, as well as the stamina and the experience about what to do when things get tough (Level 3: Enable - with knowledge, skills, and resources).

They, and they alone, are responsible and accountable for the outcome (Level 4: Empower - with responsibility and accountability). Will they return home empty-handed or with the rich food that will sustain them for the next week? And with these foundations in place, they are able to challenge and support each other (Level 5: Unleash - with challenge and support), pushing one another on to the end.

And ultimately, though it is not on camera, I am sure that on occasion some hunts fail, and after such failed hunts, there is a discussion and lessons learned so that the challenge of the next hunt will be undertaken with greater insight and experience. And there is almost certainly some elder in the camp who is able to help the group understand and work through these discussions well.

That's how humans survived and began to thrive. We use and apply this model instinctively in many situations. It is in our nature. And if we can use and apply it consciously, we can continue to thrive and grow in the 21st century with all the challenges and difficulties that life poses currently.

Executive Entrepreneur Challenge 21: Enable Your Team

This challenge is intended to force you to take action. And it is simple: set aside one hour with each of your direct reports next week to discuss what skills, knowledge, and application of these are needed to achieve your strategic priorities and goals.

(Please note that your reports should already be clear about your expectations of them because you should have done that in setting the Level 1 foundation, as outlined above. If not, use the hour to clarify Level 1 expectations and set Level 2 engagement. Then set aside a second hour the following week to look at skills.)

During your conversation with each of them about enablement, work to get clear on answers to the following questions, or variations of them:

- How is the individual doing against the expectations of his or her role and the organization's demands of him or her?

- What more support and resources does the individual need in order to succeed? If these are scarce and you can't meet the person's needs and expectations, discuss what you can do about this.

- What more knowledge and understanding does he or she need? This may not be training. It may be access to other people within the organization or even you.

Try to conclude the conversation with the simple action plan of two or three things that you and the individual can do to improve his or her ability to succeed.

Level 4: Empower - With Responsibility and Accountability

Once you've enabled your team to deliver and they are capable of delivering, then you can move on to the next stage, which is to empower them. Common challenges at this level of empowering your team include:

- *Responsibility without power:* it is no good telling someone that he or she is responsible for achieving an objective if you don't give the person the ability to do so. This may mean resources, but more fundamentally it means setting an expectation about behaviors. It is the result that you want, and there may be many different ways to achieve it. You need to give license to your staff to find the best ways that work for them to achieve their results.

- *Responsibility without accountability:* how often have you found that people set off on their own agendas either because they are not clear about what you want or because they ignored it? So fix clarity - make sure people understand what you want to achieve. Try not to spoon-feed them too much with how you want them to achieve the result because that tends to reduce their accountability. And if they going off on their own agenda, then you are going to have to find ways to bring them back on track. Reel them in a bit by reminding them of the result that you want and checking why they think their actions are in line with it - you may find something interesting in their mindset when you explore this.

Case Study: Sir Gerry Robinson

Sir Gerry Robinson illustrated the need for responsibility and accountability powerfully in his 2013 BBC documentary "Can Gerry Robinson fix the NHS?" There was a particularly powerful moment in the program that came after the hospital staff and consultants had spent weeks of time and valuable resources trying various initiatives to reduce waiting times without success. Various initiatives had failed, and wait times remained stubbornly high.

On exploring what was going on, Sir Gerry found that many of the staff knew they would fail before they even embarked on trying the initiatives. He asked the staff why they had wasted time on duff ideas. The replies were illuminating. In various different ways the staff explained that they needed to show that they were trying but that they were not committed to breaking through and solving the problem because they did not believe they were fully empowered to do so. Rather than take on the difficult decisions and accept responsibility for the outcome, they put up ideas they knew would not work in order to appear that they were trying and in order to avoid criticism.

Sir Gerry outlined carefully to the chief executive what was going on and explored what the real answer might be. It came down to one simple thing. The staff concerned needed to be fully empowered to solve the problem. They needed to be responsible and accountable for the results they were achieving. They needed to be able to make changes they knew would improve results and not to hide behind fake initiatives. It was this empowerment to achieve the results that was needed, not the request to try.

This illustrates that there is a fundamental difference between being responsible and accountable for a result and being asked just to try to achieve it. One makes people resourceful and creative, the other shuts them down. If people feel responsible and accountable for the outcome, they are much more likely to step up and find ways to achieve it. If they're not responsible and accountable, then they're more likely to be finger-pointing and finding excuses for poor performance.

So think carefully about how you assign responsibility and accountability. Are you setting your team up for success, or are you simply delegating off tasks that you don't want to do yourself? If it's the latter, then clearly you need to rethink and go back to the previous levels of this framework to make sure that you have a shared an understanding of how to enable your team to succeed.

Executive Entrepreneur Challenge 22: Set Responsibility and Accountability

The temptation here may be for you to fall back on Level 1 approaches to improving responsibility: to refine job descriptions or set down expectations in some form of written agreement, such as an email or memorandum with the staff or team concerned. Be under no illusions. If you're doing this, you are going back to Level 1 behaviors. That's fine if you think it is necessary, but this exercise assumes that you have done all that and that, therefore, something deeper is blocking the result you want. We need to explore the mindset challenges around responsibility and accountability.

Step 1: Reflect.

Take one specific goal or result that is frustrating or eluding you. Check that Levels 1 through 3 are in place and assuming that they are, get out your journal and start reflecting on what is really happening. Ask yourself the following questions:

- Do people genuinely feel ownership of the result?

- If not, why not?

- What can you do to improve this sense of accountability? How can you understand better their motivations and drivers, and tap into those, so they buy in to achieving the result?

It is often simply not enough to set financial incentives for people: they want to be inspired, engaged, and enthused. And money simply does not do that for most people.

So think deeply here and try to get to the root cause of what is going on. In most cases it will be because there is some disconnect in the mindset of those concerned, including you.

Step 2: Check in.

In much the same way as you did with the enabling task, I would like you to book some time with the key individuals concerned in achieving your goal and reflect with them on what is going on. You might do this in a more relaxed environment, perhaps over a coffee away from the office, so they open up and talk more informally and naturally about the situation. You are much more likely to get a true picture when you interact with people in this more informal way.

Step 3: Take action.

Identify two to three things from these reflections and conversations, which will make a difference in empowering people to achieve the results that you want. It might be something as simple as coaching them to step up. It might be more involved, requiring some realignment of priorities within the organization. Whatever it is, make sure it is practical and that you act upon it within the next week.

Keep going round the steps until you are comfortable that the result is being achieved. Use your journal to reflect on what you learned during this process. It can be illuminating.

Level 5: Unleash - With Challenge and Support

Many leaders move far too early towards the challenge mode of leadership without working through the earlier stages of enabling. Please don't do that. You've got to make sure the earlier stages are in place before you move on to challenge. If you don't do that and move straight to challenge, then what you'll find is you get disengagement and unhappiness, and people will start to grumble, claiming that you are unreasonable. And they will not deliver the results that you expect. So make sure the previous stages are in place before you move to challenge.

When you challenge, make sure that you do it in a supportive way. Some of what follows may be second nature to you, as it is the basis of good management and leadership, but it does not hurt to go back to fundamentals.

Here are some pointers to make sure that you are being supportive in your challenges:

- *Make sure that you understand the root of the problem*: it is not the behavior that you seek to correct but the mindset that lies behind it, to try to understand what led to the behavior.

- *Take time to reflect yourself:* have you been sufficiently clear about your vision? Have you enabled people and given them certainty that they can innovate and try things, even if they don't work perfectly the first time?

- *Ensure proximity of the result you want:* if people have no confidence that something is achievable, they are more likely to disengage than feel unleashed. What can you do to evidence that the result is achievable? How can you support your team to make this possible?

- ***Keep scanning the horizon:*** take your blinkers off for a moment and look around. What is going on that could blow you off course? Where is the market moving, and what do you need to do to be a leader in the marketplace?

- ***Leverage your position:*** in comparison to your team, you are likely to be privileged in having access to conversations, insights, and perspectives that they do not have. How can you leveraged this and share your insights with them more effectively? Similarly, how can you tap into their insights and wisdom more effectively?

- ***Pay attention to the performance of your entire team:*** there is a natural tendency to focus either on the best performers (by encouraging them further) or the worst (through challenge and support or even an "up or out" policy). I've known many leaders who pay less attention to those who are doing OK. This is a tendency that we must counter: every individual on our team is capable of greatness, so we need to find ways to bring the best out in everyone. My challenge to you is to focus on the average performers as well - what can you do to bring out the best in them?

- ***Work on your communication skills:*** how can you convey your passion and conviction more clearly and effectively? How can you avoid being abrupt or rude inappropriately? The next section will give you more pointers on this specific challenge.

Skills to Unleash Your Team

A key skill in unleashing your team is to communicate effectively, yet many of us struggle with this, both in writing, speaking, and in our non-verbal communication. Great communication is at the heart of all transformation, so if you want to make change happen, you are going to have to get savvy on this key skill. Books could and have been written about this, so I am not going to attempt that here. What I want to do is give you a few key tools and exercises that will help you hone your communication skills and get moving farther up the curve of greatness here.

Before getting into the detail, let's just understand the basics. As I have alluded to already, there are four key aspects to great communication:

- **Understanding:** before you craft your message you must understand your audience. Where are they coming from? What questions and concerns do they have? What reassurance do they need or what challenges do they need to hear as a wake-up call? You must start by understanding these questions before you start to think about what you need to say.

- **Clarity:** your message must be conveyed clearly and simply. You need to avoid highfalutin words and jargon. Speak plainly and simply to your audience in ways that they will understand and relate to. Imagine that they are outside of your organization, and you're talking to them in an informal and natural way. By setting this frame, you're more likely to speak plainly and cut to the chase.

- **Conviction:** you have to believe that what you say is important, not only to you but also to your audience. You have to convey it in a way that motivates, inspires, and encourages them to join you on the journey. If you fail to convey your passion, how do you expect them to be passionate? Take a moment before you communicate to reflect and tap into your passion. In this way you're more likely to be able to convey it to others. If it is not present in that moment, find a way to change your state so that it is present.

- **_Consistency:_** there are numerous aphorisms that remind us of this principle of communication: "Say it, say it, and say it again" and "Tell them what you going to say, say it, and then tell them what you said" are two of the most notable. The truth in these sayings should be self-evident, but it is not complete. It is not just about what you say, it is also about how you say it and how that aligns with what you said before.

Your body language needs to be congruent with your message, so hold yourself confidently while you speak, and you can be more certain that people will pay attention to what you say rather than get distracted by your nervous tics.

The challenge of aligning your communication with what you said before is not always easy to rise to. You may have changed your mind about something. You may have opened your mouth too soon in the past. Or events may be changing around you and require a different response. So I would not counsel you to echo the past to achieve consistency at all costs. That would border on insanity. Rather, what is important is that you are consistent with your own inner sense of what is needed and that you take time to explain to others why any shift in external presentation of that is different to what has happened before. Reflect on this, and your communication will be much stronger and more powerful as a result.

Think and Communicate Clearly

How many people struggle with clarifying and structuring their thinking and, therefore, appear confused and garbled in their written and verbal communications? They generate stream of consciousness words that make sense to them but which the reader or listener struggles to engage with and make sense of. Many very intelligent people struggle with this, and the world of email and speech recognition software is not improving things.

A key tool I learned here came from my time as a partner in a global consulting firm. There, we were taught to structure our thinking and written communication clearly using a standard tool which they called "top-down thinking." The chief executive was such a fan of it that he insisted all correspondence with him needed to be in this format. While I could deliver a day's training on the subject, the essence of it comes down to the discipline of writing like a journalist.

A journalist has two key jobs: she needs to grab the reader's attention and then convey her points in a way that is easy to take in, starting with the most important points first. This seems simple, but many people don't do it. So here is a simple framework for you to use.

When you are writing something, be clear about what the main point you want to get across is. Start with this, and structure your argument underneath it in blocks which substantiate the answer in sections or supporting arguments that answer the key question that your main point raises in the reader's mind. This two most powerful key questions that you should seek to raise in their mind are either "why" your main point is right or "how" you are going to achieve it. This allows you to then structure your argument in response to that key question.

You will be familiar with the "rule of threes," which consultants use: chunk your supporting arguments up into three blocks that are complete and mutually exclusive. In other words, they cover the ground without repetition.

If you can do this, you will have reached a level of clarity that will enable you to present your argument more effectively, and you can then focus on finding ways to do it with conviction and passion. Here is a template that you can use for this:

Diagram 6 – A powerful structure for communicating

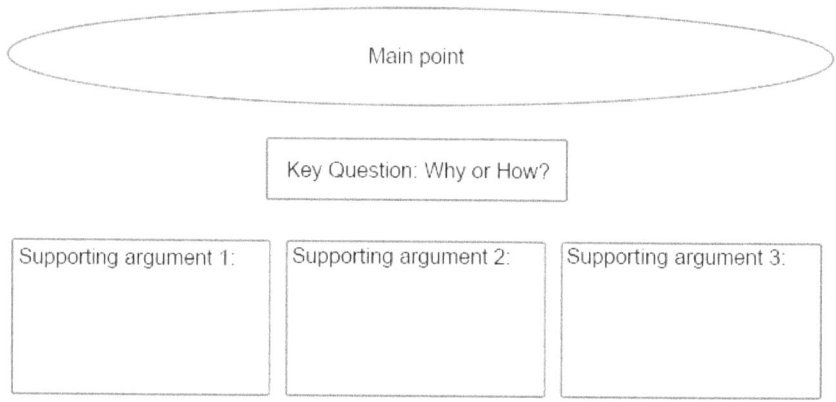

I've suggested three blocks to your argument in the template above, but you could have less or more - it really depends on what works best for you.

Coach Wisely

I mentioned above that great communication starts with understanding. One of the key tools that every good coach knows well for this is the GROW model, and I want to outline its use briefly here as a key tool for you in building understanding in driving change in your organization. It is particularly useful in one-to-one meetings where you can use it as a framework, either explicitly or implicitly, to guide your conversation.

The beautifully simple model is summarized in the diagram below.

Diagram 7: The GROW model

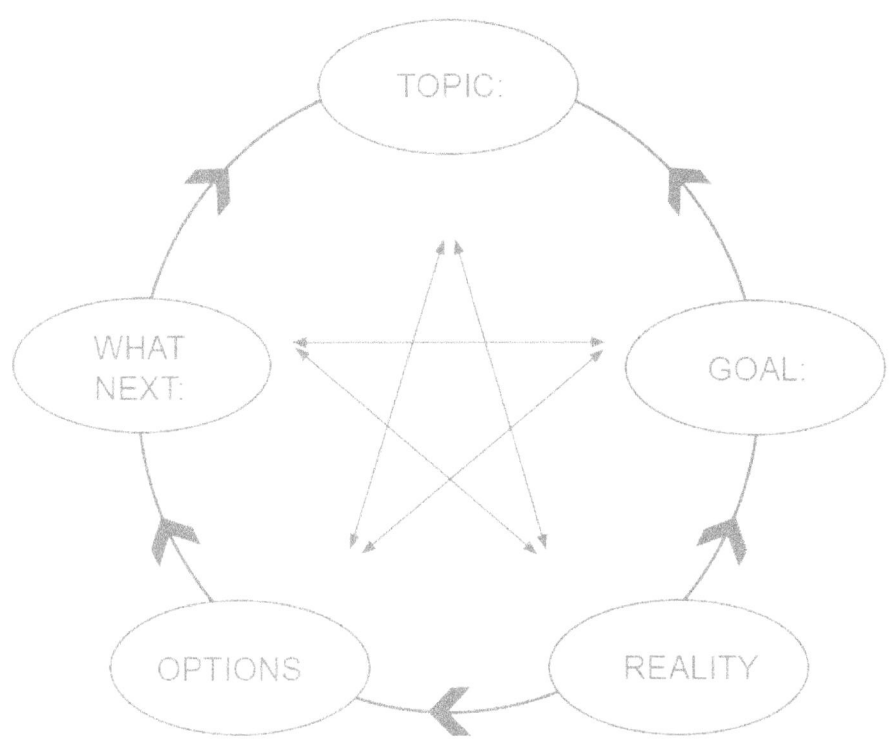

There are five key parts to the GROW model, which also follow the structure of a natural conversation. As with a natural conversation, you may want to bounce between key elements of it as you get clearer about the issue and what needs to be done about it, but it does help to follow the overall flow.

I have set this out in simple terms as follows though you should feel free to adapt the questions to make them your own and relevant to the issue or challenge you are exploring. It works as follows:

- Clarify the **Topic**:

  - What is it that you are talking about? What is the purpose of the meeting? What is the issue that you wish to discuss and clarify?

- Set the **Goal**:

  - What do you want to achieve?

  - If there is more than one goal, which one is most important? (Try to keep the discussion to one goal at a time to aid clarity and focus.)

- Understand the current **Reality:**

  - What is happening now that is relevant? Keep asking questions until the problem or challenge becomes sufficiently clear to both you and the person sitting opposite you - you need a shared understanding of the current reality.

  - Great questions here are the famous Who? How? Where? When? What? and Why? questions.

  - In addition, use open questions that get the person opposite you to dig deeper. I often ask him or her to "tell me more" or think more broadly with "Is there anything else you think is relevant?"

  - Show that you have understood the current reality by summarizing what you have heard so far. This can be a very powerful tool for crystalizing things and enabling you to move on.

- Explore the **Options**:

  - Ask the person you are speaking with what options he or she has tried or considered implementing to tackle the challenge. Explore what has worked or what might work.

  - Again, use open questions to get the person to be creative and expansive. Two great questions that I frequently use are:

    - "If you had a magic wand, what would you do?"
    - "If you were to look back in three months' time, what would have unblocked this for you?"

  - If the person is running out of options and you can see important avenues left unexplored, it is good practice make suggestions. If you are in coaching mode, it helps to ask permission to do so: "May I make a suggestion?" means that the person is more likely to be receptive to the suggestion because the person has already asked for it to be forthcoming.

  - Again, it helps to summarize what you have explored and heard. I often find that in doing so, further options and illumination enter the conversation.

  - Top tip: once a good number of options have been identified, many coaches and line managers try to move swiftly by asking, "What next?" or "What will you do?" However, the risk here is that you move too swiftly to a single solution without spending time in the Focus phase of our Scan-Focus-Act model. My advice to you is to make sure you fully explore which options are most likely to work and spend time focusing on this. Only once you are comfortable that the focus is clear, should you move to the action setting.

- Clarify What Next:

  - Once you have brought focus and clarity to the options on the table, it is time to move the conversation through to action setting. Even if you are not ready for a final decision, you need to create some momentum towards your goal. (If you are struggling here, I encourage you to reread "The General's Dilemma" and try to make a decision. You'll find out soon enough whether it was right, and you can adjust if it was not.)

  - It can be really helpful to summarize the overall decision and some immediate next steps. Midterm measures are likely to change, so focus down on what needs to happen in the immediate future to create momentum. As I have been taught: never set a goal without taking a step towards achieving it.

This is a very quick overview of the GROW model. There is a lot that could be written, and many others have done so. My aim here is to give you the basic tool and encourage you to use it within your daily communications. Don't just have it as a tool that you bring out in extremis when you feel that someone needs tailored coaching. It is a great tool for bringing clarity to a much wider range of conversations than the coaching or performance review meeting.

Challenge Constructively

Everyone knows what it feels like to be challenged or criticized unjustly or harshly. Fewer have experienced constructive challenge on a consistent basis. I believe it is our responsibility and duty as Executive Entrepreneurs to make sure that we are constructive and supportive in our challenges.

Being kind does not necessarily mean dodging the issue or being soft on a person. It means recognizing that the person or people with whom you are dealing are also human beings with thoughts, feelings, and emotions. You need to recognize them as individuals and acknowledge their efforts while demanding higher levels of performance. While we need to have high expectations and must be demanding of others if these are to be achieved, we must also respect the dignity and humanity within each human encounter. As Yeats reminds us, "Tread softly because you tread on my dreams."

There is also a great deal of common sense in the need to challenge constructively. While employees may be temporarily motivated by the desire to avoid your harsh words, most will be lifelong supporters and advocates if you adopt a constructive approach to achieving the outcomes you want. Which approach do you think will achieve more for you in the long run? If you have any doubt about the answer to this question, then you're probably reading the wrong book.

There are a few simple pointers that can help you challenge constructively:

- **Avoid responding in anger**: to be responsible means just that - to be response-able. So think carefully about what an appropriate response is. "He who seeks revenge must dig two graves" may be an appropriate phrase to bear in mind. Any form of angry response is a form of revenge. Why else would you seek to inflict your anger on someone else?

- **Be clear about the outcome that you want**: in deciding how to respond to a situation, the first question always to ask yourself is—what outcome do you want? Once you are clear about this, you can ask yourself what the best way of achieving it is. By asking these two questions, you create some space between yourself and the problem that you wish to challenge. It is in this space that the constructive challenge may take place.

- **Is it true, kind, and necessary?** These three simple questions that Wayne Dyer taught also create space between you and the issue you seek to challenge. Take a moment to ask yourself firstly if whatever you are about to say is true. Secondly, is it kind? And thirdly, is it necessary? If it passes these tests, you can be sure it is constructive. If it fails one of them, think again before deciding what to say. And don't mistake kindness and softness here. Being kind, respecting the person and having their best interests at heart may mean having a tough conversation. Just be sure it is a constructive one with their best interests at heart.

Executive Entrepreneur Challenge 23: Unleash Your TeamStep

1: Reflect.

Take half an hour to reflect on your own leadership style and where you are against this model of unleashing your teams. How can you challenge more effectively using the pointers above?

Take a further half hour to reflect now on how you measure up against all five levels of this model. What do you need to change or do in order to fully unleash your team and enable them to achieve the results you want? Try to boil this down to two or three actions that you can take this week or month to make greater progress on this.

You're not going to be able to walk in tomorrow and fix every single gap in this model all at once. So work from the bottom up. Work to establish the bottom part of this pyramid of unleashing your team. You can do that quickly and engage the rest of your team if there are problems in knowledge and skills.

Remember that it's not down to you to establish everything. Use this structure and think carefully about how you're going to apply it and stage the growth of your team so that you can move quickly towards unleashing, challenging, and supporting them to succeed.

Step 2: Teach.

What we teach we also learn. It embeds it much more firmly in our psyches. So I want you to teach at least one person in your team this system. Teach the person about the different levels involved in unleashing a team and ask them to use it in his or her own work. Take time out with the person regularly to reflect on what more you can truly do to unleash your teams. Reflect in your journal and take time to join me on the Executive Entrepreneur website to share your results.

Shift 5: Extend Your Peer Set

Part of raising your performance level comes from whom you talk to and spend time with. It is said that your performance is the average of the ten people that you spend the most time with. I don't know if there is accurate science behind this statement, but the intuitive logic of it is compelling and has proven true for me and those that I work with on a consistent basis.

If you want to play an outstanding game, with deep insights, then you need to spend more time with those who are already playing at world-class levels, both in your line of work and in other fields. This is the final key shift in raising your game as an Executive Entrepreneur. You need to implement it alongside the other shifts - don't leave it alone and expect things to get better.

By extending yourself out to others and by seeking to extend your peer set to include more people who are playing at a higher level than you, you will reap great benefits. Some of the benefits I have experienced and others with whom I have worked have found:

- *Greater motivation*: when you spend time with people who are operating at a very high level of achievement and performance, their energy, passion, and drive will seep into your psyche. It cannot help but do so if you're in any way open to them. Energy is infectious, and it will spread to you from others if you put yourself in the right situations. By sharing stories and thoughts about how they rise to their challenges, you will gain motivation and drive to tackle your own. By learning how other people have succeeded, you will gain greater certainty and drive that you too can succeed, for you are no different to them. The only differences that lie between you are in the decisions that you make.

- **_Deeper insights:_** you have probably experienced this in your own career. If you look back on times when you were achieving at your best, you will have had great people around you, whether that was inside or outside your own organization. You will have shared ideas and thoughts and passions with them. And the conversations that you have with them will have generated new insights and greater drive. Intelligent people who are successful will be more than happy to share thoughts and ideas if you're with them in the right place at the right time. These people will be busy, so you're going to have to find ways to spend time with them that are natural and fit with their routines and pressures as well as yours.

- **_Introductions to people who can help:_** if you widen your circle of friends and share your challenges and opportunities with them, you will find that people are more than happy to make introductions to others who can help you if they can. It is in most people's nature to want to help other people that they know, like, and trust. If they think that an introduction they can make will benefit both parties, then why would they not do so? Your job here is simply to put yourself in close proximity to others who are succeeding at high levels and then to find ways to be helpful to these people alongside sharing your challenges and opportunities.

Know Your Nature

Are you by nature more of an extrovert or introvert? Understanding this will help you as you seek to extend your peer set. So you want to spend a bit of time examining it.

The first thing to understand is that an extrovert is not necessarily the person who is the life and soul of the party that spends all the time talking away and telling people how great he or she is. And the introvert is not necessarily the wallflower who shies away from social contact. These are traits we associate with the words "extrovert" and "introvert," but for the Executive Entrepreneur, you need to think of introversion and extroversion as meaning something quite different.

An extroverted Executive Entrepreneur will be at her best in a group setting, with one or more talented people to share ideas with and bounce things off of. The energy and drive that other people bring to the table is important for her. She works best by sharing her ideas and building on them with others, or even discarding her own ideas when other people come up with better ones.

The introverted Executive Entrepreneur will prefer to work through the problem alone in a quiet room and think through all the angles herself before exposing it to other people for scrutiny and challenge. The introvert is more self-sufficient and prefers to clarify her own mind first. She does not need other people to tell her whether she is right or wrong.

That is not to say that the introvert does not like or need other people - it is just that she is less dependent on them to know within her own mind what the right answer is. And she is less in need of other people to help her tap her own inner drive and get going when the going is tough.

All people have both traits in them. Neither is good or bad: it just depends on how you use the trait and leverage it to your own advantage and the advantage of your business.

My advice is to build on the strengths of your dominant character trait, be aware of the weaknesses, and moderate your behavior where appropriate to take account of these.

If you are predominantly an extrovert by nature, you will want to build on the following strengths:

- ***Problem-solving with others:*** use brainstorming sessions and team meetings to work through problems. Quick problem-solving sessions with others can produce insights very quickly and help you move forwards more rapidly. Bringing in experts from outside your organization can help you gain even more insight and clarity to the problems. Recognize and celebrate this character trait, for by using it you will bring others with you and make your journey more certain.

- ***Getting things done:*** the extrovert prefers to work as part of a team or as the leader of a team. Put others around you who can help you succeed and leverage their talents to help you do so. Coach and develop them as you drive to deliver. By tapping into their talents, you are going to be much more likely to succeed.

But be aware of and moderate the following weaknesses:

- ***Needing others to succeed:*** if you don't have enough high-caliber people around you, as an extrovert you may struggle to carve the success that you yearn for. This can be particularly hard for the small business owner or the self-employed, but also for the senior executive. The higher up the organization you go, the fewer people you have to confide in. It can be lonely at the top. The best way of moderating this weakness is to put in place a power network of people you can share thoughts and ideas with as you go forwards. We cover this in the exercise below.

- **_Attention to detail:_** many extroverts are not completer-finishers and struggle to pay sufficient attention to detail. You can moderate for this character trait, firstly by recognizing it. While "good enough" may be acceptable to get things moving, you might want to find someone who can cast an eye over the detail and think through the pitfalls before you charge into battle. The "black hat" way of thinking that Edward De Bono identifies as one of his six hats is useful here: think critically about what could go wrong and consider what you can do to handle these pitfalls. Again, use your journal: carve out ten minutes of quiet time to think critically about the issue you're tackling and what you can do about it. Write down your thoughts and find two or three actions that you can take, which will help you pay attention to the detail.

- **_Ignoring quieter people:_** the extrovert may be tempted to forget people who are quieter or gloss over the smaller contributions they make. This can be a fatal flaw, both in teambuilding and in ensuring that you take people with you on your journey. Moderate for this behavior by being conscious about it. Look for the views of quieter people, and if they are not forthcoming in open session, find quieter moments in which you can draw out their thoughts and insights. Be aware of body language: closed posture, folded arms, looking away with eyes, for example. When you notice these, pause and ask yourself what you can do to bring a more open response. Those who are quieter are just as valuable and their insights maybe just what you need, so spend a moment in meetings when other people are talking and look around. Ask yourself if everybody is engaged and find ways to draw in those who have not yet contributed fully.

If you are predominantly an introvert by nature, you will want to build on the following strengths:

- **Staying focused and getting things done:** one of your great strengths as an introvert is that you filter out distractions well and you are able to stay on task and keep going. Build on this strength by using the peak performance tips outlined above: in particular, work in ninety-minute chunks with no distractions, and you will see great results come through.

- **Finding your own way through tough challenges:** the introverted character needs less from other people in working through problems and finding answers. This can be a great strength if you are resilient and keep working away at the challenge at hand. Success rarely goes to the most brilliant, but rather to the most persistent. Thomas Edison was said to have found thousands of ways that did not work before he invented the light bulb, for example. So be persistent and resilient, for this is one of your great strengths.

But be aware of and moderate the following weaknesses:

- **The grand reveal:** one of the introvert's tendencies can be to work away on a problem, find the right solution, and then fail to socialize it with others before critical meetings. I remember well one junior executive who had spent a month putting together a proposal that would transform ways of working with the new organization. He'd crafted a well-argued proposal with strong evidence and a clear plan for the way forward. He presented it confidently at a management team meeting and was deeply surprised when the proposal was rejected. The chair of the management meeting took him aside afterwards and explained: nobody in the management team had been involved in the crafting of his proposal, nobody understood it, and nobody was behind it when it had been presented. The young executive took note and vowed never again to present a proposal with a grand reveal.

- ***Splendid isolation:*** it can be a temptation to think that you can get things done without the need to take other people with you. The higher up in organization you go, the less true this is. So I expect that most readers of this book will need little coaching on moderating this character trait. But it is still something to be aware of. Many of the organizations I work with complain of silo behavior, and some of their leaders lack the insight and ways of working needed to get cross-team exchanges actually working. One of the root causes of this is the failure to moderate for introverted behavior.

  If you are leading a project or initiative in your organization, think broadly about whom you need to involve. It won't just be those within your line command. You will need to work across the silos or the matrix that the organization has created and in which you operate. Push yourself beyond your comfort zone. Reach out to others outside your line of command who can help you get things done. Spend time with them at the water point or over a coffee. Get to know their agendas and priorities. Understand them as people, and you will build a much stronger platform for delivering your change.

- ***Thinking other people don't need you:*** a final weakness I want pick out for the introvert to pay attention to is that introverts often think that others around them are doing just fine. They may not realize that people are struggling or would welcome their help and input. They project their own sense of inner strength and confidence, and often fail to be sensitive to the fact that other people need support. They may misinterpret brash and confident behavior in others as a sign that they are not needed, when actually those people may be much in need of support, even if just a quiet word on the side. Don't fall into the trap of thinking that other people don't need you. Reach out to them, ask them how they doing, and explore their challenges. Don't be afraid to offer your insights. You have a ton of experience that will be useful to others, and the vast majority of people will be grateful that you have taken an interest in them.

In this way you can build a much more powerful network of supporters within your organization. Passing your support forwards will bring it back to you tenfold.

Executive Entrepreneur Challenge 24: Leverage Your Nature

Take a blank two pages of your journal and draw a horizontal line across the middle of the page so that you have four quarters.

Step 1: Explore your character traits.

At the top of the left-hand page, write "extrovert," and at the top of the right-hand page, write "introvert." Above the horizontal line, write down examples of your ways of working that fall into either extroverted or introverted behavior. This will give you a clearer sense of what your dominant character trait is if you did not know already. More importantly, it will give you a clearer sense of the strengths that you need to build on and the weaknesses that you need to moderate for. Be honest with yourself in this first step of the exercise, writing down both the good and the bad examples of your ways of working that fall into the particular trait. And remember that we have both traits within us.

Step 2: Identify ways to build on or mitigate your character traits.

Below the horizontal line on your page, brainstorm ideas for building on the strengths and mitigating the downsides of the character trait, with a view to strengthening the likelihood that you will achieve the outcomes that you want for you and your organization.

From this long list, identify two or three things that you can do in the next week. Put these actions into your diary if you can. Allocate time to making sure that they happen. So for example, if you're naturally introverted, you might allocate time to networking across your organization and spending time with people that you don't normally spend time with. Or if you're naturally extroverted, you might allocate some quality time for yourself to think through problems.

Step 3: Reflect and improve.

At the end of the week, look back on this page that you created and reflect more on what you have learned from taking the actions that you identified in step two. What have you learned? What do you need to do differently going forwards? If this exercise has benefited you, why not schedule sometime next month to reflect even more and build on what you have learned?

Listen to Your Customers

One of the risks in driving through any business development or growth is that you take an internal perspective on things. You look at things from your own perspective and fail to take account of the views of your customers. The first rule of service improvement is to listen to the voices of your customers. Understand what they want and need, and design services and improve them to respond to those needs.

I worked with a team in a software company that, until I worked with them, had tried to manipulate the voices of their customers because they wanted to keep things simple for themselves. They had their own view about what was important and how to manage their scarce resources, and their customers' needs and priorities were secondary to the views of the team managing the design and building of the software.

They picked points from what their customers were saying, which substantiated their priorities, and ignored the other voices. They thought they understood better than their customers. And they wondered why they had unhappy customers and why, as a result, they struggled for scarce additional internal resources to improve their software.

As soon as they engaged with their customers and sought to incorporate their views and priorities into the development of the software, a totally different perspective on priorities emerged. The company was able to prioritize much more effectively and lobby for additional resources to drive change much more effectively, simply because they started to engage their customers fully, rather than nod sympathetically and take note of the complaints they received.

Another organization I worked with took the opposite approach. Movember identified customer champions for the design and delivery of their service improvement program called True NTH. I led the UK end of this work for three years.

We worked with a number of patients and clinicians to design projects to change the face of prostate cancer care, and we placed the voice of the customer - the man with prostate cancer - at the heart of this work.

By putting men at the heart of the program, we incorporated an incredibly powerful and honest force for change into our work, and the results showed through in improved health care pathways that are being taken up across the country and shared with leaders around the globe.

Executive Entrepreneur Challenge 25: Listen to and Involve Your Customers

You may already have initiatives in hand to listen to the voice of the customer, so you may choose to adapt this exercise to incorporate those, but if you don't, this is a simple way to get started.

Step 1: Identify key customers to involve.

Look across your customer base and identify four or five key customers that are significant users of your service. Ideally, these are not just customers that you know and love. Think also of customers who are more demanding and challenging. By bringing such customers closer to you, you will find more ways to improve your services.

Step 2: Invite these customers into your organization.

While you may not want to give away all your inside secrets, try to find ways to involve these key customers in the design and delivery of your products or services. Let them help you prioritize and shape the improvements you are thinking about putting in place. You'll often be surprised about how insightful and helpful this can be in winning over other people inside your organization.

Step 3: Share the results.

Once you have improvements to show as a result of involving your customers, share these both with those people and internally, but also celebrate the results more widely. Share your customers' experiences with others and use this to help you drive wider marketing and understanding of your services. Strong customer advocates can make a huge difference in the performance of your marketing efforts.

Look Outside Your Organization

One great way of extending your peer set is to look outside your organization. The most recognizable way of doing this is by appointing non-executive directors. CEOs and boards frequently look to people outside the organization to bring fresh perspectives and additional insights to the challenges they face in growing the business. This is a great way of extending your peer set, but it is not the only way. And particularly if you're not in a position to appoint a non-executive director, you need to explore alternatives.

Other ways that you can increase your peer set include:

- **Including external people on your project board:** good project boards always have a customer (or user) and a supplier involved. Think both about your supply chain and your customer base as you establish your project board, and make sure that you bring these voices to the table. They will be incredibly valuable to you in understanding any blocks and challenges that you are sure to encounter as you design and deliver your project.

- **Establishing an external advisory panel:** an advisory panel is common in the research world, where administrators of funds often don't have the deep specialist knowledge needed to sort out the good research proposals from the bad. But it is not only researchers that can benefit from external advisory panels. I've seen such mechanisms used to great effect in government organizations and private sector companies too, as part of a customer advocacy program. They are a very powerful way of leveraging experience and wisdom that you don't normally have access to. And the external advisers are often happy to sit on such panels for the kudos and recognition that they bring.

- **_Identifying coaches and mentors_:** external coaches and mentors can be a great way to bring in outside expertise and knowledge in a laser-like manner. You can identify key individuals that will benefit from mentoring or coaching, bringing the help for a defined period of time and with a specific outcome in mind. This has the benefit of building the skills and competence of your team, and avoids the rather more costly approach that many resort to of hiring an external consultancy team. I cover how to find great coaches and mentors in more detail below.

- **_Join a coaching group:_** a really great way of extending your peer set is to join a coaching group, a set of like-minded individuals from different organizations all seeking to raise their game that a coach has assembled. By joining such a group, you gain the expertise and wisdom not only of the coach but also of the other people within that coaching group. And the friendships forged last well beyond the duration of your membership in that coaching group.

Executive Entrepreneur Challenge 26: Extend Your Peer Set

In this exercise I want you to look outside your organization for experts in the field you are tackling. Take a specific project or challenge that you are working on and think about who else you can involve outside your organization.

Step 1: Describe the skills and expertise that you need.

List the skills and experience that you need from people outside your organization. Think carefully about the perspectives that could benefit you. Don't worry too much at this stage if you don't know of people with these qualities. That's for step two. At this stage I just want you to get clear on what it is that you want and need to bring in from outside.

Step 2: Identify people with those skills and expertise.

Once you've identified the type of person you want to involve, think about whom you already know that fills that requirement. If it is the voice of the customer, think about who your best and most vocal customers are. If you don't know who these people are, then ask someone in your organization who does.

If you need a specialist and you don't know such a person, do a bit of research: who has written about the subject? Who is blogging regularly on it? Don't be afraid to reach out to these people: why else do you think they are blogging or writing about it? An alternative is to look for referrals: ask people you know if they have access to such an expert. LinkedIn is great for this, as well as picking up the phone or dropping somebody a quick email.

The bottom line is that there is a wealth of expertise out there, and many people will be more than happy to share it with you, provided there is some return for them, whether it is because it helps their careers, improves their kudos, or fits with their business.

Step 3: Invite them into your project or program.

Once you have identified relevant people to involve, the next step is to ask them. Do so with clarity: be clear about how you are going to involve them and the benefit to them. Provided you have asked intelligently, you will get the result you are looking for.

By extending your peer set in this way, you will bring fresh challenges and perspectives to your business, and you push yourself and your business forward faster than otherwise would have been possible.

Invest in Coaching and Mentoring

If you go to the gym and work out, you get fitter. If you work out with a physical trainer, you get fitter faster. If you work out with a world-class physical trainer and you are a world-class talent yourself, you are likely to reach the pinnacle of your potential. This is simply because the trainer is going to push you harder than you will push yourself on your own. It's why all the top athletes have coaches, and it's something that you need in your own professional setting as well.

Most leaders of large businesses and organizations these days have experienced some form of coaching or mentoring. And yet it is still relatively uncommon in the ranks. I think this is one of the key weaknesses in corporate learning and development.

Without coaching and mentoring, how do you expect to attract and develop world-class performers? And how do you expect them to be motivated and driven to succeed at ever-higher levels? And how do you expect to retain them when their enthusiasm and passion begin to flag?

So if you don't have a coach or mentor, you need to think very seriously about getting one. My view is that everyone should have a coach or mentor. They provide new ideas, hold you accountable, and push you towards new limits. What ambitious person thinks that he or she does not need this help in life? Show me such a person, and I will show you a person who is not yet achieving his or her full potential.

Some people ask me about the difference between coaching and mentoring. In my view, coaches know how to get the best out of you.

They don't necessarily need to understand your business and industry well, at least at the outset of the coaching relationship. But they need to have quick and inquisitive minds, and be able to get to the bottom of the challenges that you face, working with you to understand the blocks and what to do about them.

Here is a simple checklist of things to look for in a good coach:

- **Track record:** coaches will have worked with other people of a similar or higher position than you. They will have built up their experience over time and will have great reviews from people they have coached and worked with.

- **Inquisitive and quick mind:** you want to find a coach who can get to the root of the problems and challenges you face. You probably know a lot more about the situation you're tackling than you give yourself credit for, so a good coach should be able to dive into your perspective and ask great and inquisitive questions to get to the heart of the matter quickly. By asking these questions and by holding an independent frame of reference, the coach will help you get perspective and quickly identify what you need to do in order to move forwards.

- **Ability to challenge and push you beyond your comfort zone:** like any great physical trainer, good coaches will expect you to be able to achieve more than you're already delivering. They will not necessarily take your first answer and assume that it's right. They may challenge you to think again and think more deeply about what you can do to raise your game. You need to welcome this challenge and embrace it because this is what will take your game to the next level.

- **An introductory offer:** it may seem obvious, but it's worth mentioning that a good coach will not seek to take money off you before you and the coach both know that you are a good fit for each other's styles and ways of working. A good coach should give you at least one, if not two, free coaching sessions to experience what it is like to work together before asking you to commit to a paying relationship.

A mentor, on the other hand, is someone who has tackled a similar challenge in the past and who knows how to solve it because they have first hand experience of doing so, even if in a different environment. Mentors also bring their own skills and experiences to the table and share these with you as you work together on the challenges that you face. Mentors will often have less time to share with you than coaches, but their contacts and industry knowledge can be invaluable.

Here are things you can look for in a good mentor:

- *Wisdom and experience:* a good mentor will have a long track record of tackling and solving problems similar to the ones that you are facing. The mentor will put new ideas in your head and inspire you to achieve them.

- *Contacts:* a mentor should be willing to share his or her contacts with you in order to achieve the results that you want. While you may not ask this upfront, it is something to be aware of as you explore the mentoring relationship.

- *An open and giving nature:* your mentor should be willing to help you even if there is nothing much in it for him or her (as opposed to a coach, where rightly a financial arrangement is needed to enable the coach to live). The fact that the mentor has been there in the past means that he or she should understand the challenges that you're facing and, if you found the right person, should want to help you through these.

I've also been asked what makes the difference between good coaching and great coaching, and it is worth spending a moment on this. Great coaches will often do two further things:

- **They will combine coaching with mentoring:** great coaches will combine their coaching expertise with their wisdom and experiences of delivering in the work place. They won't be non-directive, passive mirrors of your anxieties and challenges. They will help you explore your challenges by bringing some of their own knowledge and insights to the table. They will do this with your permission and in a sensitive way, rather than flooding you with nothing but their own ideas. But their experience does give them additional insight that you should tap into to accelerate your progress. Learn from the best, and you stand a better chance of playing at their level.

- **They will assemble coaching groups:** great coaches will put together a range of other people working to achieve their goals. While these people may have different professions, they share similar ambitions and appetites for success. In these coaching groups, people learn from each other as well as from the coach; and they learn as they see and help other people solve a wider range of problems than they might normally come across in their own work situations. One board member I worked with who had been part of such a high-level coaching group remarked that he had made years worth of progress due to the situations he had worked on in helping other people without having to leave his day job. In this way, everybody wins. It's a much, much more powerful way of developing yourself than just doing one-on-one coaching or mentoring.

In my Executive Entrepreneur program I bring together great leaders from different walks of life, and together we work on the challenges that we face and help each other achieve amazing results. And, as I explained earlier in this chapter, you will lift your game because you are rubbing shoulders with a wide and talented peer set.

You will gain from their insights, inspirations, and breakthroughs. Your performance will start to lift, and you will start to drive yourself to greater heights. It's a powerful experience to be part of a coaching group. And because at least some of your coaching is done in a group setting, it makes the investment more affordable.

If you have not already experienced working in a coaching group, I would encourage you to find an opportunity to do so, whether in the Executive Entrepreneur program or another opportunity.

It is a fantastic way to learn, grow, and extend your peer set, all wrapped up in a single, coherent experience focused on your needs.

Success Tip on Coaching - Don't Hesitate

The Kalahari bushmen I have talked about in this book operate successfully in one of the harshest environments in the world. Their story reminds me of a different and more tragic story where a journalist exploring the Nile lost his life because he ventured into a similar environment without appropriate support. He was fairly experienced and understood the harshness of the desert environment, but tragically it turned out he was not quite experienced enough.

As he journeyed into the desert, he began to feel ill, and the early signs of heat stroke were not picked up until it was too late to get medical assistance. Within three hours he had collapsed and died. This was recorded as part of a documentary about the Nile and reported on TV. Talk about reality TV.

While this is an absolute worst-case scenario, and my thoughts go out to the family of the journalist concerned, it does serve as a harsh reminder to the wise. Whenever you are in a harsh environment, whether for business or pleasure, make sure you have the best support available and ensure that you are prepared and resourced to make that journey quickly and safely. Check and recheck yourself, and pace your progress to a rate that can be sustained.

The business world can be a jungle, particularly in this day and age of digital marketing with hundreds of different offers, products, and vehicles at your disposal. Make sure you have the best support and advice possible to get you through that jungle and out the other side, intact and in great shape.

Listen to your instincts and your intuition. If you're get a feeling that things aren't right, then listen to these signals. Check what is going on and make adjustments if necessary. It is OK to adjust. It is OK to change your mind. You can seek expert support.

You are not alone. Don't sacrifice your goals because you are not prepared to reach out to others for help or make adjustments to your course of action. Focus and act persistently and consistently towards achieving your goals. And reach out if you need help. The worst thing you can do is not to try.

Executive Entrepreneur Challenge 27: Find a Coach, Mentor, or Coaching Group

At the risk of over-coaching, I have set this as the final challenge within this book. If you have not already experienced great coaching or mentoring, then it is about time that you did.

The Internet abounds with coaches these days, but my advice is not to start there. Talk to people around you. Ask them if they have had a good coaching experience, and if so, ask for a recommendation.

Alternatively, or in addition, please do consider joining one of my Executive Entrepreneur coaching groups. They are an affordable and powerful way of giving you a high-quality coaching experience, and I would be delighted to have the opportunity to work with you as you seek to take your journey as an Executive Entrepreneur to the next level. You will get extra insights and much more value out of this workbook if you work through it as part of a coaching group. Find out more about the coaching groups and the option of one to one coaching at *http://www.theexecutiveentrepreneur.com*

Take Your Journey Farther!

Download your FREE workbook, join one of my coaching groups, meet like minded individuals, and work through challenges together!

Find out more at:
www.theexecutiveentrepreneur.com

Chapter 5 - Putting It AllTogether

My aim in writing this book has been to give you a framework you can apply in real time to boost your own performance and that of your team. It is a practical framework and one that will work for every Executive Entrepreneur. I know because I apply it myself and help others to do so.

In this final chapter my aim is not to give you more tools and techniques to bolster your practice. Rather, it is to get you to reflect, engage, and take action on what you have learned. So I want to leave you with a few key thoughts that I hope serve to galvanize you and encourage you to take action on your journey as an Executive Entrepreneur.

Knowledge Without Action Is Useless

Knowledge without action is useless. And yet even the smallest of actions, when applied daily, will stack up over time. Faith can indeed move mountains if applied intelligently and persistently to drive one's actions.

Think about this for a second, and you will see that it is true. When Kennedy announced that he would put a man on the moon, it was a leap of faith, albeit a carefully calculated one. It captured the nation's imagination and focused great minds and resources on achieving the goal. It required many smaller steps to be taken, and many breakthroughs were achieved along the way. But the persistence and focus with which NASA and other organizations tackled the tasks at hand were clear. Together the faith of a nation did more than move mountains: it established a great step for mankind.

Ghandi is another luminary in this regard. His persistent and consistent evocation of nonviolence eventually led to the freedom of a nation, casting off the shackles of colonial rule. His well-known periods of fasting drew the nation together and called them to a higher purpose. The smallest of actions on the part of one man created a tsunami within the nation that no colonial power could hold back.

And the list goes on. Think of any great leader and what defines them. Fundamentally what defined them was consistent and coherent action focused on something they held dear to their hearts. While they may not use the Executive Entrepreneur framework consciously, you can see its structure and power in everything that they did - Mandela, Mother Teresa, Ghandi, Abraham Lincoln, and so many more.

If you're not in the habit of reading biographies, I encourage you to do so and to start with luminaries, such as these. They will inspire you, and you must remember that they are exactly the same as you. The only difference lies in the decisions that they made about how to focus and act on their convictions.

We Don't Have All the Answers, Ever

It is mistake to think that we have all the answers to the challenges we face in life. We rarely do. What we have is resourcefulness. We know that we can apply ourselves to the problems we face and find a way through. We advance rather than retreat; we grow rather than stay within our comfort zones. We rarely have all the answers. What is important is that we engage in trying to find them.

Again, the truth of the statement should be self-evident, but I know many executives struggle with feeling that they have to be totally in command because for think being in command means having all the answers. To these people, I encourage recollection of the story set out in "The General's Dilemma." Departments of analysts can struggle to find the right answer to a complex question. Often in these situations it becomes important simply just to act.

I've written about the importance of engaging your heart. One common challenge I have found in the coaching I do is that people struggle to find their sense of purpose and the conviction that they can realize this purpose. While the exercises in this book, particularly those around engaging your heart, will help you if you're still struggling with your true purpose, your inner calling for your area of expertise, then rarely will greater, deeper analysis help you. What will help you is taking action. By starting to move down a certain road, you will find if it is right for you. There is no shame in deciding later that you want to take a different road, but you must remember that there really is only one road and that is the one that you are on. Start journeying down it one step at a time.

Balance

Times of change and growth are stressful, make no mistake about that. We may enjoy the action, the challenges, and the thrill of the chase, but we must recognize that these place a certain degree of stress on our minds and bodies. And if we focus on nothing but the goal, we lose sight of the views and experiences we gathered along the way. We must remember that it is the journey rather than the goal that brings us into contact with people and gives us joy and satisfaction. We never truly reach our destinations unless we enjoy the journeys on the way.

Just as we may enjoy going to the gym and pulling muscles under stress and strain, so we must also ensure that we feed our bodies well and take appropriate rest. If we did nothing but go to the gym and work out intensively for forty hours per week, our minds would be a wreck, shattered by the stress and weak beyond compare. It is the balance between rest, nourishment, and exertion that make us stronger and fitter for future challenges.

So it is with your journey as an Executive Entrepreneur. Find your inner balance. Stay focused and centered on your goal, but take your blinkers off from time to time to enjoy the view. Remember that the people around you are on their own journeys. Take time to know and understand their journeys, for they will help you on yours.

Better Never Ends

The steps outlined in this book will drive the expanding and upwards spiral of performance that you seek. As you scan, focus, and act, if you are drawing on the insights and expertise that your coaches, mentors, and extended peer set can offer you, you will achieve levels of performance you previously thought were out of reach. And the exciting bit about this journey is that once you reach one level of excellence, the journey continues. A whole new vista of opportunities and challenges will arrive, and you will be called to rise to these. Better never ends!

One of the fundamental principles of any improvement program, any relationship between a mentor and a tutor is, that they know that better never ends. Even greater heights lie beyond, and that is my hope and prayer for you as you work through this book - that you take these principles and techniques in here and use them to fuel your successes both in this year and beyond.

If I can be of help on your journey, please do reach out. I am easy to find. And I wish you well in all of your endeavors.

Take Your Journey Farther!

Download your FREE workbook, join one of my coaching groups, meet like minded individuals, and work through challenges together!

Find out more at:
www.theexecutiveentrepreneur.com

Bibliography

Attenborough, David. "Persistence Hunting: Human Mammal, Human Hunter," from episode 10, "Food for Thought," in The Life of Mammals BBC natural history series. Released on 5 February 2003. Youtube video clip, 7:09. Accessed on 8 February 2016. https://www.youtube.com/watch?v=826HMLoiE_o.

Branson, Richard. Screw It, Let's Do It: Lessons in Life. Australia: Random House Australia, 2006.

Can Gerry Robinson Fix the NHS?. London: BBC, 8 January 2007. Television series, two seasons and four episodes.

Collins, Jim From Good To Great: Why Some Companies Make the Leap… and Others Don't. Random House Business Books London, 2001

de Bono, Edward. Six Thinking Hats. New York, NY: Little Brown and Company, 1985.

Fleming, Eric. Don't Think About Purple Elephants. CreateSpace Independent Publishing, 2012.

Frankl, Viktor. Man's Search for Meaning. Boston: Beacon Press, 1959.

Ghandi, Mohandas, K. An Autobiography: The Story of My Experiments with Truth. Boston, MA: Beacon Press, 1957.

Isaacson, Walter. Steve Jobs: The Exclusive Biography. New York, NY: Simon and Schuster, 2011.

Kahneman, Daniel. Thinking, Fast and Slow. New York, NY: Farrar, Straus and Giroux, 2011.

Mandela, Nelson. Long Walk to Freedom: The Autobiography of Nelson

Mandela. Randburg, South Africa: Macdonald Purnell, 1995.

Parnin, Chris. "Programmer Interrupted." Ninlabs Research (blog). 19 January 2013. http://blog.ninlabs.com/2013/01/programmer-interrupted/.

Robbins, Anthony. Unlimited Power: The New Science of Personal Achievement. New York, NY: Free Press, 1986.

Rohn, Jim. The Art of Exceptional Living. Read by author. Simon and Schuster Audio/Nightingale-Conant Corporation, 2003. Audiobook, 6 compact discs.

Rumelt, Richard. Good Strategy Bad Strategy: The Difference and Why It Matters. New York, NY: Crown Business, 2011.

Russell, Bertrand. Conquest of Happiness. New York, NY: Horace Liveright, 1930.

Ward, Rachel. "Oprah Winfrey: A Career Timeline," The Telegraph. 23 February 2011. http://www.telegraph.co.uk/culture/tvandradio/8343834/Oprah-Winfrey-a-career-timeline.html.

Yeats, William Butler. "Aedh Wishes for the Cloths of Heaven," The Wind Among the Reeds. New York, NY: J. Lane, The Bodley Head, 1899.

About the Author

 Kevin is a business consultant and a qualified coach, specializing in helping people just like you to transform and grow their business. He's worked with a wide range of leaders over the last 20 years, including secretaries of state, chief executives, entrepreneurs, business owners and a wide range of senior executives. Following a career as a high-flying civil servant, he worked as a management consultant in KPMG and Capgemini. He reached the equivalent of partner as a member of PA Consulting's Management Group before setting up his own consulting and coaching business, where he now specializes in business transformation and growth.

He has lead national and global change programmes, corporate mergers, project turnarounds, cost reduction drives and nine figure investments in service transformation. He is what the Harvard Business Review calls a "triple strength" leader, having deep experience of driving change across public, private and not-for-profit organisations.

His clients know the world is changing and that they need to adapt their services and products, perhaps even their whole organization, in order to survive. But they are also tired of surviving and want to thrive.

They have big ambitions and want to implement them quickly. They may also feel that they lack sufficient clarity, resources, time, knowledge or a combination of all of these.

They need someone to help them break through these challenges so that they can establish the business that they desire.

Kevin loves helping people through these challenges and sees his job as enabling his clients to succeed and thrive. He offers a variety of coaching and training programs and also provides tailored business consulting services for larger organizations. You can find out more about his work at *http://www.therealkevinrennie.com*